SELF - DEVELOPMENT FOR SUCCESS

# Influencing people

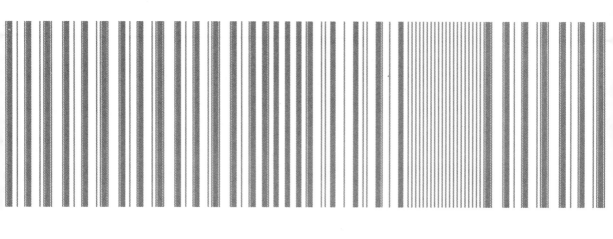

## Acknowledgements

There are several writers and thinkers whose work have influenced me in writing this book, notably Peter Senge, Chris Argyris, and Stephen Covey. The quiz on pages 26–30 has its origins in a number of similar matrices developed by writers and researchers, such as Tannenbaum and Schmidt, Blake and Mouton, Thomas and Kilmann and, Stephen Covey.

I owe a debt to the many clients who have helped me understand what genuine influencing is and who have also provided the opportunity to work with them on refining their skills. I also thank my colleagues and associates at Management Futures, particularly my fellow director, Phil Hayes, for their invaluable assistance and expertise on this topic.

SELF-DEVELOPMENT FOR SUCCESS

# Influencing people

THE ESSENTIAL GUIDE TO THINKING AND WORKING SMARTER

# Jenny Rogers

AMERICAN MANAGEMENT ASSOCIATION

**AMACOM**
American Management Association
New York • Atlanta • Boston • Chicago • Kansas City
San Francisco • Washington, D. C.
Brussels • Mexico City • Tokyo • Toronto

A Marshall Edition
Conceived, edited, and designed by
Marshall Editions Ltd.
The Orangery, 161 New Bond Street
London W1Y 9PA

This book is available at a special discount when ordered in bulk quantities. For information, contact Special Sales Department, AMACOM, an imprint of AMA Publications, a division of American Management Association,1601 Broadway, New York, NY 10019.

This publication is designed to provide accurate and authoritative information in regard to the subject matter covered. It is sold with the understanding that the publisher is not engaged in rendering legal, accounting, or other professional service. If legal advice or other expert assistance is required, the services of a competent professional person should be sought.

Cataloging-in-Publication Data available.

Printing number

10 9 8 7 6 5 4 3 2 1

Series Consultant Editor  Chris Roebuck
Project Editor Conor Kilgallon
Design  Joanna Stawarz
Editorial Director  Ellen Dupont
Art Director  Dave Goodman
Managing Art Editor  Patrick Carpenter
Managing Editor  Clare Currie
Editorial Assistant  Dan Green
Editorial Coordinator  Rebecca Clunes
Production  Nikki Ingram

Cover photography  The Stock Market

Originated in Italy by Articolor
Printed and bound in Portugal by Printer Portuguesa

# Contents

# 1

## Introduction
## Why influencing matters
## Influencing and
### 'emotional intelligence'

# Golden tips

# Control as an illusion

# Introduction

Influencing effectively is the one core skill that every leader and manager needs. In a business environment, there is no other skill that so clearly separates the competent from the merely average or obviously inept performer. You may be a brilliant strategist but unable to persuade people to accept your strategic ideas. You may be an outstanding financial controller but lack the spiel to persuade people to follow your system.

Influencing is also a core life skill. If you have it, you will be able to manage most of the challenges your business and personal life present.

Consider these situations. They all require skill in influencing:
- ■ Asking a boss for a pay rise
- ■ Telling a small child that it is bedtime
- ■ Dealing with a team member who is underperforming
- ■ Persuading a colleague to accept your ideas
- ■ Rebuilding a relationship with a partner after a disagreement
- ■ Negotiating an important sale in a way that safeguards your interests

- ■ Asking for a discount when making a major purchase
- ■ Presenting your side of the story when accused of doing something wrong
- ■ Briefing your team about changes which may be unpopular.

## Not just a business skill

All the previous points describe situations in which the other person is likely to have strong views and the outcome clearly affects both parties. In each case, the cost of influencing ineffectively can result in long-term financial problems and damaged relationships.

Influencing is not just a business skill; it may be even more significant and challenging in your personal life. It could be said, for instance, that if you can regularly persuade a small child to go happily to bed, then you can do anything in business!

In effect, influencing is the sum total of many skills which fall under one label. In this book, all the different skills are carefully dissected. To achieve all of them requires consummate skill – certainly challenging but clearly achievable – with dedication and practice.

# The golden tips for influencing

There are some definite do's and don'ts where influencing is concerned. Some of them are counter-intuitive; that is, they appear to contradict common sense. All are explained in more detail, but a handy list of hints, are presented for you below.

Just as there are some 'must-do's' for influencing, there are a number of behaviors to avoid. If you ignore these "don'ts", you can be sure you will not achieve the desired outcome.

## Influencing 'do's':

1. Put your main effort into trying to understand the other person. Ninety percent of the time, influencing goes wrong because we put all our effort into expounding on our own views

2. Listen, and show you are listening, by using the skills of summarizing and clarifying

3. Know yourself: understand how you appear to others; recognize your own unhelpful 'hot-buttons' and work on eliminating them

4. Ask open questions and listen carefully to the answers

5. Create authentic rapport with the other person through using appropriate body language

6. Let people find their own solutions. Develop alternatives to giving others advice

7. Develop a range of styles appropriate to the occasion – don't just rely on one or two ways of influencing

8. Stay open to being influenced yourself. Ask for feedback and learn from it

9. Act on the belief that you have the right to be heard and to say what you want

10. Create common ground through your enthusiasm and your focus on the positive

## Influencing 'don'ts':

1. Starting with a fixed position that you are determined to defend at all costs; 'telling it as it is'

2. Shouting, yelling, screaming and finger-jabbing

3. Interrupting the other person with your own views

4. Talking more than you listen

5. Relying on facts, figures, logic and data as the most compelling part of your argument

6. Being determined not to be influenced by the other person

7. Making assumptions about the other person's motivation

8. Never asking for, or paying any attention to, feedback

9. Giving advice

10. Leaving other people to guess what you want

# Why influencing matters

**P**eter works in the City. He deals with brokerage houses and is responsible for implementing some of the regulations that apply to them. Apparently he has a lot of influence. But Peter feels frustrated. He has frequent meetings with senior people from the brokerage firms but comes away without getting what he wants. "They do everything they can to undermine me," he says. "It's subtle but very obvious to me. They do it by just ignoring a lot of what I suggest or by using delaying tactics. I could force them to do things; but, if I do, the whole situation will get worse."

Jan manages a team for a well-known chain of food stores. She is making buying decisions that affect prices and products, and she has a lot of discretion over what she buys. Yet Jan, too, is puzzled by what is going wrong. Her team resists her ideas, to the point where it has its own team meeting before she holds *her* meeting. Team members explain this by saying that they have things to discuss that would bore her, but Jan is convinced that they use this time to "conspire" against her. She may be right. She explains this away by telling anyone who asks that this is a team of very clever and highly independent people; so anyone in her position would

have this problem, wouldn't they?

Peter and Jan have authority over their teams and colleagues, yet they are not in authority and lack influence. What is going on here?

## Changes in organizations

Part of what is happening is that organizations are in very different places than they were only twenty years ago. Listed below are the five main ways in which the business world has become more streamlined, more sophisticated, and more competitive.

### 1. The disappearance of the middle manager

The over-managed organizations of the late seventies and early eighties have been transformed, mainly by a reduction in management levels. In one public-sector organization, for instance, there used to be no fewer than 39 different management grades. These have now been reduced to just six. This is usually described by executives as "introducing a flat hierarchy".

*Result: Fewer people have more to do, with larger spheres of influence.*

## 2. Lean is mean

Organizations have also become leaner and smaller. Whereas, in previous years, it was possible to hide in an organization until retirement, now it is not.

*Result: Poor performance is more visible than it was. If you are a manager, under-performance may be associated with an inability to work with people, i.e., an inability to influence.*

## 3. The rise of the customer

Organizations have had to become more customer focused in order to survive. Customers rightly expect to be treated with respect. Not doing so ensures that their business will go to a competitor. Customers may not always be right, but it is fair to say that no one ever won an argument with them.

*Result: The skills of dealing with customers have become a prime arena for influencing. People without these skills find themselves at risk.*

## 4. Working across organizations

Some problems seem to defy solution. A good example is the so-called *winter pressures* issue, where hospitals can experience a sudden upsurge in demand in severe weather. In some cases it looks as if the hospitals are blaming the elderly patients who have nowhere else to go ("bed-blockers"); the social services staff blame the hospital; and the patients blame their families or the voluntary agencies.

There is probably sufficient money and resources available to solve the problem, but only if everyone involved comes together and ignores the usual boundaries and power struggles.

*Result: Collaboration can solve problems that power alone cannot. Collaboration requires influencing skills.*

## 5. The death of authority

Unthinking deference to authority figures is now a thing of the past. Education encourages us to think for ourselves; television and other kinds of mass communication, such as the Internet, have demystified previously remote figures, including politicians or very senior managers. If a well-known person is guilty of an indiscretion, it is highly likely that the world will know of it sooner rather than later.

*Result: No one, however grand, powerful, or senior, can rely on traditional authority to make other people carry out orders. The only real alternative to traditional authority is influencing.*

# The pointlessness of control

Skill in influencing is vital for another reason. Leadership in modern, successful organizations is about persuading, not about telling people what to do or giving orders. This is hard if you have been brought up on old-fashioned authoritarian ideas of "command and control."

Even in the most desperate situations, human beings can resist control. One of the most moving books to come out of World War II was Victor Frankl's remarkable work, *Man's Search for Meaning*. Frankl was a young doctor when he was sent to a concentration camp. Life in the camps meant being stripped of all status, being cold and weak, hungry and living with the daily threat of death. Frankl survived and described his decision *not* to submit to the powers that were threatening to rob him of his inner freedom. He concluded that, even when faced with the horrors of camp life, it is really up to each of us to decide our own mental and spiritual fate.

## Applying the example

In the very much more mundane and everyday world of being a manager, it can help to realize that control is an illusion. It is worth noting that:

- It is impossible to force people to work effectively on something they disagree with. People have literally thousands of ways of resisting, all of them effective: resigning, strikes, leaking to the press, absenteeism, "presenteeism" (physically present but mentally absent), sabotage, mute resistance, complaining, mockery, open rebellion, public compliance, and private contempt.
- Organizations are so complex and subject to so many diverse forces that it is pointless to try to control them.
- The distance between the top and bottom of the hierarchy, even where it has been much reduced in length, makes it unlikely that the most senior members could ever truly control the most junior.
- Much of the control exercised by organizations is unnecessary: for instance, peers can and will manage time-keeping and vacations in organizations where there is openness and willingness to give feedback.
- Control reduces risk-taking, a necessary precondition for the innovation on which organizations depend for survival.
- Attempts to control are exhausting: they sap energy from more important aspects of leadership.

# Influencing and 'emotional intelligence'

There has been considerable interest recently in what makes exceptional managers tick. What is it that distinguishes them from the herd? The answers seem to be that, while, they are probably bright (but often no more so than many of their contemporaries), what they have is "emotional intelligence" (EQ). This is the ability to manage human emotion skilfully – one of the prime factors in influencing.

A recent study by 3M, one of the most consistently impressive companies in the world, showed that where there had been performance problems, in only ten percent of cases were failures in technical know-how to blame. Ninety percent of the time the cause was lack of "emotional intelligence," including the ability to influence others.

Research on the use of so-called 360-degree feedback in organizations has consistently shown that, in managers rated as outstanding by their colleagues, there is a high correlation between their own and their colleagues' ratings. In others words, the best managers have a clear view of who they are and a realistic view of how they appear to others. The least effective managers are those who rated themselves higher than their colleagues did.

EQ means that you know yourself. You know exactly what your own "hot buttons" (the things that make you angry quickly); are and, equally importantly, how to control them. You will know that certain types of situations and certain types of people are likely to bring out the best or the worst in you. If you have EQ, you will recognize your patterns and be adept at controlling your responses to them.

## Knowing others

At the Bell Laboratories think tank in Princeton, a study was made of what made outstanding performers. These turned out to be people who had high EQ and the ability to:

- Build rapport
- Network effectively
- Work effectively as a team member
- Build consensus
- See things from others' perspective
- Be persuasive
- Deal with conflict

All of these qualities are associated with being able to recognize emotion in other people and then being able to manage it. The person without EQ doesn't notice that a team member may be boiling with rage. The person *with* EQ does and can produce an appropriate response.

The lesson from this research is that it is not enough to be good at the task side of your job. You must also be good at working with people. And this means that you have to know how to influence them.

Knowing others is intelligence; knowing yourself is true wisdom; mastering others is strength; mastering yourself is true power.
(Lao Tze)

# 2

## What is influencing?
## Concentrating influence
## where it matters

The problems of advice

Push and pull levers

Circles of Influence and Concern

# What is influencing?

**Successful influencing means:**
**Getting a result that meets the legitimate needs of both sides.**
The word legitimate is important. It is not a legitimate need, for instance, if you have a gunman holding a planeload of passengers hostage, and he asks for fuel to fly the plane to another airport.

It is a legitimate need if a team member asks you to OK having a vacation in August because his children have their time off from school then. It is legitimate for you to think this may not be a good idea if everyone else in the team is also away and there is continuing demand for your services as a team.

**Achieving results which stick.**
Influencing, which seems to get a good result at the time but which is not sustained, is not effective influencing. For instance, if you and a member of your team agree that she will redo a piece of work and she then reneges on the deal, you have failed as an influencer.

**Improving, or at the very least, not damaging the relationship between the people involved.**
This is where the *might is right* style of influencing always fails. People may appear to agree. They may appear compliant. But over time, the cracks begin to show. A boss who forces a team member to do his or her bidding may achieve a short-term gain, but in the longer term the employee will have the last word – by leaving, by complaining, or by inflicting damage in some way. When one side has been forced to do something, a relationship of trust is destroyed and will be very hard to rebuild.

## INFLUENCING IS NOT:

- **Forcing others to accept your point of view**
- **Continuously nagging until they agree**
- **Bargaining**
- **Giving in to someone else's view even when you believe they are morally wrong**
- **A debate**

## Giving advice

It's very easy to confuse influencing with advice-giving. Here are some situations where influencing is needed:

- A member of your team approaches you about a project she is working on. She knows you have more experience in the subject of the project and asks, "What would you do?"

You can see that a colleague is getting into difficulties with his drinking. He's in the bar every lunch hour and again after work. People are beginning to talk about the smell of beer that hangs around him. What would you do?

## The easy answers are:

- Tell the young member of your team how you would solve the problem; after all, she has actually asked you for your experience.
- To take your colleague aside and tell him that drinking is damaging his health and his reputation. He should control his alcohol intake and, if he can't do that, then he should get some professional help.

## The likely results

But let's look a little more closely at what would be likely to happen if you gave the above responses.

- With the team member, she gets her answer and the problem appears to be solved. But in the longer term, she has not done any thinking of her own, and you are reinforced in her mind as the person with the answers. Her own ability to develop has been curtailed.

With the colleague, it is unlikely that he doesn't already know he has a problem with his drinking. He is probably worried about it and its causes. Giving him advice may mean that he does it in less public places, rather than controlling his drinking.

## The pointlessness of advice

As opportunities for influencing, it is probably safe to say that neither of these interventions on your part is likely to be successful. You may feel better, but the underlying issues have not been resolved.

Think about something you do yourself that is unwise, such as smoking. Now, imagine that a friend is giving you the standard advice on this subject. For instance, he or she might tell you that every cigarette shortens your life by five minutes; that smokers are twice as likely to develop heart, lung and circulatory disorders; and that smoking is highly antisocial.

How does this advice make you feel? Have you ever had advice of this sort which has actually produced a change in your behavior? The most probable answer here is "no."

We all do things that are unwise:
- Driving too fast
- Eating a high-fat, low fiber diet
- Being overweight or underweight
- Drinking too much
- Working too hard

How do you feel when you have been given advice on any of these topics? You are likely to feel defensive, angry, and even more determined to resist.

## What is influencing?

**POSSIBLE RESPONSES TO ADVICE:**

Advice does not work as an influencing tactic for these reasons:

- It suggests that the advice giver is wise and sensible, while the advice recipient is a rather sad case who cannot get his or her life together.

- The recipient's energy is focused on repelling the advice, rather than on dealing with the issue itself. This leads inevitably to the "Why don't you...? Yes, but..." game:

  "Why don't you get more exercise? It would really help you to reduce the stress."

  *"Yes, I agree it would be a good idea; but I don't really have time."*

  "OK, why don't you cut down on the hours you work?"

  *"I'd like to, but my boss won't be satisfied with less than the amount of time I'm giving now."*

  And so on and so on.

- Advice giving discourages people from taking responsibility for themselves. If they take your advice, it is *your* ideas, not their own, they are following.

- It does nothing to develop people's resourcefulness and resilience. If they take your advice and it goes wrong, then it becomes "your fault."

## Getting to the heart of the matter

If you give advice, it is unlikely that you will be telling the other person anything they have not already thought of for themselves. For instance, advice on health and lifestyle issues is all very widely available. The reasons that people smoke and drink unwisely have little or nothing to do with the unavailability of information on the subject.

When we give people advice it can come from wanting to avoid the pain of getting to the heart of the issue with the other person. It can also make us feel wise and helpful when it is possible that we are neither. Giving advice can happen for good and bad reasons. The positive reason is that we want to be helpful. The less worthy reason is that we want to control the other person through the mechanism of giving advice.

## Other traps

The first is our tendency to read our own biography into the situation other people are describing:

*"Could you give me some advice on how I ought to deal with my boss?"*

*"Oh yes, I remember when I had a difficult boss, I…"*

The problem here is that you can never know what it is like to be the other person. Your responses were yours alone. The truth is that you *can't be* the other person, and ultimately, you can never know what it is like to be them.

In situations where you are tempted to give advice, consider instead the much more powerful techniques of genuine influencing in the rest of this book. Some powerful alternatives to advice are to listen, to summarize, and to ask skilful questions. Some especially useful questions to pose in situations where people ask you for advice are given in the section on page 50.

## The levers of push and pull: the core skills

Influencing involves six core skills, all of which are described in this book. These skills fall into two categories, sometimes described as "the levers of influence." The first three are "pull" skills, which are associated with finding out from others what they really want and what they are thinking. These pull skills are creating rapport, authentic listening, and asking skilful questions.

The second set of skills are called "push" levers; they establish what you think should happen. These include asking for what you want, saying no when appropriate, and giving feedback.

Many people are a lot better at the pushing than pulling. What can happen here is that when two people who are both good at pushing get together and

## What is influencing?

put forward equally strong and vehement views, they quickly get into mutually reinforcing destructive behavior.

Take a typical meeting. James is suggesting ideas for an advertizing campaign to Tara, a colleague on the same team. They have been asked to work together to prepare a proposal for a client. James strongly believes that television is a pointless medium for the product the agency has been asked to promote, because so few people from the age group at which the product is aimed actually watch TV. Also, he points out that TV is considerably more expensive than the highly targeted posters he believes will have greater effect.

Tara feels that a poster campaign would be like a scattergun and thus far less effective than TV. Also, she enjoys working with TV more than she enjoys working with posters.

### No influencing achieved
The meeting takes the following form:
James: "I want to do it my way."
Tara: "You're wrong; let's to do it my way."

This takes about an hour of increasingly bad-tempered discussion. Both make nods to the other, saying versions of, "I hear what you say…" followed significantly by versions of, "But, I think my way is better." As a conversation, neither side has influenced the other in any way, and the working relationship is likely to be fraught with tension for some time to come. It has become a struggle for control, and both people are even more deeply embedded in their views than they were at the outset. Furthermore, each thinks the other is stubborn, arrogant, and wrong.

Neither has listened to the other, and their vehemence simply creates more opposition.

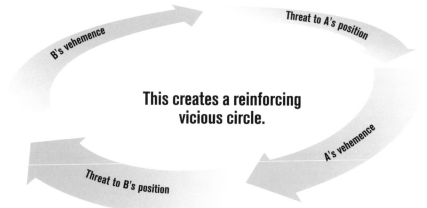

B's vehemence

Threat to A's position

**This creates a reinforcing vicious circle.**

A's vehemence

Threat to B's position

The martial arts of the Far East have much to offer here. In martial arts, you use the force of an opponent to unbalance and surprise. The basic philosophy is that, if you push directly, you simply create more force against yourself. John Heider's wonderful translation of the *Tao of Leadership*, first written thousands of years ago in China, puts it well:

- If a group member wants to fight with you, consider the strategy of the guerrilla commander. Never seek a fight. If it comes to you, yield, step back. It is far better to step back than to overstep yourself.

- Advance only when you encounter no resistance. If you make a point, do not cling to it. If you win, be gracious. The greatest martial arts are the gentlest. They allow an attacker the opportunity to fall down.

## Striking a balance

Balancing push and pull usually leads to a more creative solution and to lasting, nondamaging agreements.

Also, a different kind of conversation is possible. In the example opposite, Tara could first try finding out what James really thinks. Why does he feel that TV would be pointless? Tara should be listening hard at this point. This, paradoxically, will make her a much more effective influencer because she will learn a lot about *how* James thinks. She should then summarize his views to make sure she really understands them; and, only then, should she offer her own views, assertively. Tara should then pause to check how her views are being viewed. Again this seems paradoxical, as it appears to invite James's disagreement; but it is far more likely to result in James listening to her, for the simple reason that he is being listened to.

If they still don't agree, Tara should draw attention to the areas of disagreement, but should also try to find out what they do agree on. Throughout the conversation, she should be alert to her own, as well as James's reactions, paying most attention to the emotional, rather than rational, element of the argument. Rationality is only skin deep, and to influence people we have to be alert to our own and others' hot spots.

These are high-level skills, especially when you are discussing something you really care about. More time is devoted to developing these skills later in the book.

# Concentrating influence where it matters

The techniques of influencing require discrimination to use. There is no point in trying to use them in situations where they cannot make any difference. The American writer and management guru Stephen Covey makes a useful distinction between your "Circle of Influence" and your "Circle of Concern", below.

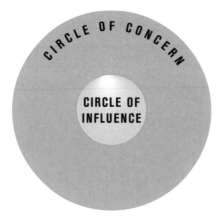

## The two Circles

In the Circle of Concern are all the things we worry about, but over which we have no control – the possibility of nuclear war, climate change, Third-World poverty, and so on. In the Circle of Influence are all the things we *can* change – essentially our own attitudes and behavior. It is all too easy to concentrate effort on the Circle of Concern. In my work as a consultant, I see many clients whose energies are engaged in pointless complaining about the

mistakes of others. "This government is ruining our chances of competing overseas"; "My boss is making my life intolerable"; "Another recession is making it impossible for us to earn a decent living."

## This victim mindset has several consequences:

- Feelings of powerlessness
- Development of low self-esteem
- Becoming unable to take control
- Becoming the target of bullying

It's a hard lesson to learn, but the only areas you can be certain of changing are the ones within your own circle of influence – and that means your own behavior. Other people are responsible for their behavior, and you are responsible for yours. You cannot make other people responsible for yours.

## Give-away language

If you tend to concentrate too much on your Circle of Concern, look out for phrases like this:

- If only they'd… (do something that would make my life better)
- If I just had…(time/ money/ resources)…everything would be all right.
- If my partner didn't do x or y (our relationship would be easier).

You can influence other people's behavior by changing your own; but if you set out to change them, you are doomed to failure. The client who said to me, "I can't understand why my team doesn't listen to me" was falling into this trap. My reply was, "You mean everything would be all right if only they'd listen to you?" He realized with a grin that the issue was what *he* was able to do, not what *they* should do.

A basic and useful principle here is, if what you're doing isn't working with someone else, change what you're doing; don't try to change the other person.

## Increasing the Circle of Influence

If you direct your energy more fruitfully, the relative size of the Circle of Influence increases, and the size of the Circle of Concern decreases, as shown in the figures on the right. Eventually the Circle of Concern becomes completely engulfed.

The way to do this is by increasing your skill in using the techniques of influencing – again, concentrating on what you can do to change your own behaviour instead of feeling like a victim of what others do.

Here are some ways of reframing your language to avoid concentrating on your Circle of Concern:

| INSTEAD OF SAYING: | TRY SAYING: |
| --- | --- |
| ▪ If only my partner would... <br> ▪ If only I had more time... <br> ▪ Life in this organization is horrible. If only they'd... <br> ▪ You get discrimated against in this organization if you're a woman. | ▪ I can do x or y to change what I do. <br> ▪ I can manage my time differently. <br> ▪ Life really is horrible here. I can make it better for myself by... <br> ▪ I can find work where my gender is not an issue. |

# 3

## Self-assessment
## Interpreting the results

The five influencing styles

The drawbacks of each style

Self-awareness

# What's your typical influencing style?

**W**hen we need to influence another person, most of us tend to have a favorite style. To use a metaphor from computers, we have a "default" mode, the one we tend to rely on most often. Of course, when the occasion demands it, we can use other styles, but we may not use them as frequently as is really necessary. In fact, it is more likely that, when we are under stress, we will revert to our favorite style again.

This is probably not a good idea. Everyone needs a range of styles and to be able to use them flexibly. If you always use one style, it is likely that you will elicit the same response from others, regardless of

## Style A

| WHEN TRYING TO INFLUENCE SOMEONE, I TYPICALLY: | ✓ Yes, this describes me |
| --- | --- |
| Enjoy a debate. I get a buzz from it | |
| Put my own point of view across vigorously | |
| Take the lead in a group | |
| Like having the last word | |
| Feel strongly motivated by the need to reach my goals | |
| Speak up when I think I'm right | |
| Get annoyed by people who won't stand up for themselves | |
| May annoy others by seeming bossy | |

| AND OTHER PEOPLE MAY DESCRIBE ME AS: | |
| --- | --- |
| Forceful | Confident |
| Abrasive | Ruthless |
| Articulate | Determined |
| Impatient | Inflexible |

the situation. Skillful influencing requires the ability to use a range of different styles as appropriate.

Try filling in this questionnaire. Go through all the questions, checking any of the statements or descriptions that you agree describe your behavior or opinion. Try not to think too long about any one answer; give the answer instinct tells you is right. There are no right or wrong answers.

Check those statements that describe you. Leave the box blank where you think it doesn't.

## Style B

| WHEN TRYING TO INFLUENCE SOMEONE, I TYPICALLY: | ✓ Yes, this describes me |
|---|---|
| Explore conflicts in order to defuse them | |
| Coax the other person to express their views before sharing mine | |
| Create rapport with the other person | |
| Feel strongly motivated by a need to share power | |
| Invest as much time as a process needs | |
| Like being a facilitator | |
| Get annoyed by people who refuse to work as equals | |
| May annoy others by over-elaborating the process of influencing | |

| AND OTHER PEOPLE MAY DESCRIBE ME AS: | | | |
|---|---|---|---|
| Patient | | Steady | |
| Long-winded | | Over-serious | |
| Calm | | Willing to learn | |
| Impassive | | Afraid of failure | |

## What's your typical influencing style?

## Style C

| WHEN TRYING TO INFLUENCE SOMEONE, I TYPICALLY: | ✓ Yes, this describes me |
|---|---|
| Put other people's needs first | |
| Make it easy for others to confide in me | |
| Keep myself open to influence from the other person | |
| Have skill in listening | |
| Feel strongly motivated by a need to create harmony | |
| Like being the "glue" in a group | |
| Get annoyed by aggressive people | |
| May annoy others by refusing to ask for what I want | |

| AND OTHER PEOPLE MAY DESCRIBE ME AS: | |
|---|---|
| Cooperative | Modest |
| Passive | Fearful of authority |
| Flexible | Unselfish |
| Cautious | Lacking authority |

## Style D

| WHEN TRYING TO INFLUENCE SOMEONE, I TYPICALLY: | ✓ Yes, this describes me |
|---|---|
| Go for the practical outcome | |
| Look for tradeoffs: give a bit, get a bit | |
| Live for the moment; tomorrow is another day | |
| Talk my way out trouble | |
| Feel strongly motivated by a need to find immediate solutions | |
| Like being the troubleshooter | |
| Get annoyed by people who stick to protocol and rules | |
| May annoy others by giving in too quickly | |

| AND OTHER PEOPLE MAY DESCRIBE ME AS: | |
|---|---|
| Pragmatic | Focused on the short term |
| Cynical | Tactical rather than strategic |
| Charming | Optimistic |
| Frivolous | Naive |

## Style E

| WHEN TRYING TO INFLUENCE SOMEONE, I TYPICALLY: | ✓ Yes, this describes me |
|---|---|
| Ask the difficult questions about things that could go wrong | |
| Prefer to leave the really hard decisions to others | |
| Identify with the underdog | |
| Avoid getting competitive | |
| Suggest getting extra information before making a decision | |
| Feel strongly motivated by wanting to avoid being the target of other people's anger | |
| Like being the person who seeks underlying causes | |
| Get annoyed by people who deliberately create conflict in relationships | |

| AND OTHER PEOPLE MAY DESCRIBE ME AS: | | | |
|---|---|---|---|
| Sceptical | | Discerning | |
| Fearful | | Suspicious | |
| Careful | | Low-key | |
| Procrastinating | | Unconfident | |

## Scoring

There are 16 possible points for each style, one point for each check you have put against the 16 different questions.

Now, add up all the checks for each of the five different styles to give yourself a score; and put the totals in the boxes below:

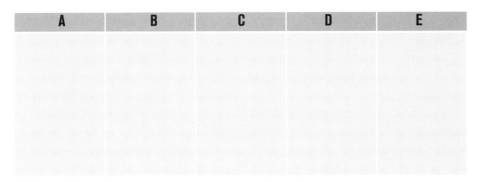

| A | B | C | D | E |
|---|---|---|---|---|
| | | | | |

## What's your typical influencing style?

This questionnaire is based on the idea that when you set out to influence someone, there are two forces at work:

- How much you try to meet your own needs
- How much you try to meet other people's needs

**This creates five basic styles of influencing:**

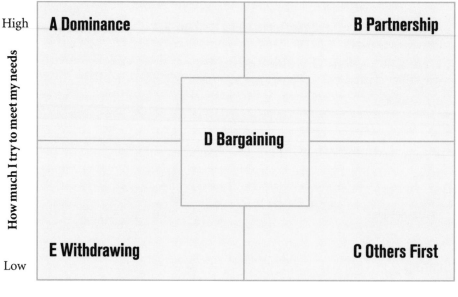

Interpreting the quiz

**Interpreting the quiz**

Your favorite style and the one you rely on is the one where you have most checks.

Your back-up style is likely to be the one where you have the second highest number of checks.

If you have roughly the same number of checks in all the styles, you may be able to use them equally and with versatility. On the other hand, you may be giving people a confusing impression, and they may not be sure where they stand with you.

Your least-used style is likely to be the one with the smallest number of checks.

Each of the styles has its advantages and disadvantages, though to be effective as an influencer, you should be able to make use of all five styles. However, there will probably always be one or two that you can use more easily than the others.

# What the styles mean

### Style A: Dominance

When you adopt this style, you put your own needs first and take less account of the needs of others. It is useful when the situation calls for unequivocal leadership. It means speaking up – for instance, for a cause you believe in, or when it is important for others to know exactly where you stand. It's also the style to use when there isn't time for debate. For instance, if the office you are working in is on fire, the firefighters simply order people to leave; this is not the time or place for discussion or negotiation.

In general, you probably believe that it's more important to be right than to be liked and find it relatively easy to make unpopular decisions. Many business leaders prefer this style. The traditional boss believes that people need to be told because they do not want to take responsibility for themselves.

### Downsides of style A

- It can create fear, one of the main barriers to productivity at work.
- It can create resistance. This may show itself in a number of ways, ranging from outright rebellion to subtler forms of subversion, like absenteeism, all of which absorb too much energy.

### If this is your dominant style you may find that:

- People avoid trying to influence you because it's too frightening or takes too much energy.
- You get cut off from feedback or any kind of bad news and may therefore have an inaccurate picture of how other people see you.
- Other people see you as good at the technical aspects of your job, but not so good at the people side.

If this is your style, you should look particularly carefully at the sections in this book on the 'pull' levers of listening, questioning and creating rapport.

## What the styles mean

### Style B: Partnership

If you adopt this style as your dominant approach to influencing, you will place a high value on a collaborative approach. You also will believe that it is possible to achieve outcomes in which what you want and what the other person wants can be met in equal measure. You will be willing to spend time exploring the other person's views, even when these include uncomfortable feedback about yourself.

It is the style to use when it is important to create healthy, long-term relationships where neither side feels exploited. It is also the style that's most appropriate where the long-term goals are clearly defined and are critically important to both sides.

Style B may seem like the desirable ideal, and many business books do point it out as the most effective; but watch out – it has downsides, too.

### Downsides of style B

■ It assumes that there is unlimited time for influencing and persuading, whereas, in reality, there may not be.
■ It assumes that the other person is as committed as you are to a true partnership of equals. This may not be the case, and you could find your own good will exploited by a more ruthless opponent.

**If this is your dominant style, you could find that:**
■ You are expending energy trying by seeking a win-win outcome, when the matter under discussion is too trivial to justify the time and effort you are devoting to it.
■ Other people see you as constantly seeking to spread risk, or even to avoid responsibility, by trying to make a partnership out of every situation.
■ Others are prepared to take advantage of your good will.

If this is your preferred style, you should look very carefully at the sections in this book on asking for what you want, saying "no," and giving feedback.

## Style C: Others first

In this style, you place others' needs high, and your own low. You may sometimes see this style described as lose-win; that is, you lose, and the other person wins. This style is useful when you are trying to develop other people's confidence; for instance, it might be a tactic you use when you are trying to develop a team member through delegation.

It may also be appropriate to show unselfishness in the interests of preserving or maintaining an important long-term relationship.

It may be a useful style when the topic under discussion does not involve deeply-held values, or where the issue is not earth-shattering for you.

In general, you probably believe that it is more important to create harmony between the members of your team than to have your own way, simply because you are the boss, and that people will probably see you as an excellent listener.

### Downsides of style C

- You may find it difficult to make tough, but necessary, decisions.
- By holding back your own views you will probably miss opportunities to influence others.

### If this is your dominant style, you may find that:

- People assume you will always go along with what they want. You may end up feeling resentful because your good will is exploited.
- You get bypassed for jobs that require dynamic leadership.

If this is your style, you should read the sections on the "push" levers, such as giving feedback, asking for what you want, and saying "no".

## What the styles mean

### Style D: Bargaining

The overall flavor of this style is the give-and-take of compromise. You give way on some of the things you want and expect the other person to do the same. This style is useful when each side knows that the relationship is short-term and no great principles are at stake. It may also be appropriate when the goals are unclear and will only emerge after time has passed. This style was typical of industrial relations in the 1970s, when trade unions and employers seemed to have equal bargaining power; and neither side was able to identify common ground. Here, you can see another advantage of the compromise style: both sides were able to talk about the outcomes as "victories" by emphasizing what they had gained and minimizing what they had lost. If this is your dominant style, you probably enjoy the rough and tumble of influencing and pride yourself on your ingenuity, charm, and ability to respond well to a crisis. This is the style of the natural trouble-shooter.

### Downsides of style D

- You may look for compromise when it would be more appropriate to stick to your principles and to devote more time to the process of influencing.
- You may seek compromise when it is more appropriate to give in.

### If this is your dominant preference where influencing is concerned, you may find that:

- You get outmaneuvred by people who appeal to principles.
- You give in too easily and too soon.
- People see you as willing to sacrifice important values for the sake of a pragmatic solution.

If bargaining is your preferred style, you should learn all the "pull" and "push" techniques explained in this book.

## Style E: Withdrawing

This style can be useful when there is danger in making a hasty decision that could have disastrous long-term consequences. For example, when there are important gaps in information, it may be better to withdraw.

It is also a sensible approach to adopt when you are faced with overwhelmingly powerful opposition, and the best option is to keep your head down.

If withdrawing is your dominant style, you will probably be able to raise doubts about the viability or correctness of any proposed solution and may also see real dangers, which everyone else ignores.

This is the style of the naturally cautious influencer.

### Downsides of style E

- Your low-key style may mean that people simply forget to consult you on certain issues.
- People may misinterpret your concern with what could go wrong as lack of courage.

### If this is your dominant style, you may find that:

- Important decisions that may concern you are made without your input.
- You end up looking and feeling like a bystander.
- You may find the "rebel" position attractive because it seems easier to criticize, than to take part.

If withdrawing is your preferred style, you should study both the "pull" and "push" sections of this book, as these techniques could add to your portfolio of useful styles.

### Self-awareness

The necessary first stage for greater effectiveness is self-awareness. You need to identify your typical patterns – the behavior you rely on and possibly overuse, and the behavior you avoid, including behavior that could be useful.

To increase your range and diminish the impact of unproductive patterns necessitates new awareness, dedication, and practice. These are the subjects covered in the rest of the book.

# 4

**The "pull" skills of influencing**
**Creating rapport**
**Genuine listening**
**Asking questions**

**Summarizing**

**Testing your assumptions**

# Creating rapport

Creating rapport is the most fundamental skill of all and the foundation skill of the "pull" levers. You cannot influence someone if you have not established rapport with him or her.

A client of mine – I'll call him Michael – asked me for help on managing his team. "I don't know what's going wrong," he said. "People tell me I'm intimidating. That's not what I intend at all. I'm a pussycat, really. But I sometimes see people deliberately getting up to avoid me when I come into the open-plan office. What can I do?"

Talking to his team revealed some immediate answers to his question. Michael is an unusually tall man, as well as very senior in his organization. When he came into the open-plan office, he would approach people and lean on their desks while talking to them. He has a strong voice and he loves to discuss whatever is on his mind at the moment.

## Negative body language

His behavior had several effects on the other person. It emphasized his height. They were still sitting down, while he was standing up. The enormous difference in height underscored his seniority, and his loud voice came across as dominating. His wish to enjoy an on-the-spot discussion simply made people feel they

were being interrogated. The total impact was overwhelming. Michael was not getting what he wanted from his team because he simply didn't know how to create rapport. He had no idea how he came across; and, when he was told, he didn't know what to do instead of what he was doing.

With another client, there was a different problem. Gail had difficulties getting her team to take her seriously. When I met her, I immediately saw one reason why. In our entire initial conversation, lasting perhaps an hour, Gail had only made eye contact three or four times. The rest of the time, she looked just above or beyond my chair or at the ceiling. The cure here was very simple. Gail's lack of eye contact suggested either shyness or that her attention was elsewhere. Therefore, her team read this as lack of the confidence and indifference to them and to the team's business. Learning to break the habits of thirty years and to look people in the eye was difficult but had a radical effect on Gail's relationships.

## Positive body language

Look at a rather different situation. Here is a team that gets along well. Its numbers are discussing future strategy. If you videotaped them, you would notice that everyone is sitting in roughly the same way. All are crouched and leaning forward intently in their chairs. All the chairs are at the same angle to the table. There is a lot of nodding and careful listening. This team has established rapport.

## Managing your body language

Try this experiment. Ask a friend or colleague to talk to you about something they really care about for about two minutes. Warn them that about half way through, you will be subtly diverting your attention – for instance, by slightly looking away or looking at your watch – and that you will then bring your attention back to them. I ask participants in the courses I run to do this as an activity. It always has the same result. The people who are talking simply cannot continue. They always dry up, even though they have been warned about what will happen.

## Mismatches

When you are mismatched someone (that is, when your body language conflicts with the other person's), you cannot have rapport with them; and it is therefore unlikely that you will be able to influence them effectively. Have you been guilty of any of these in a conversation in which you needed to influence someone?

| ACTIVITY | IMPRESSION CREATED |
| --- | --- |
| Fiddling with your watch, pen or ring | Looks as if you are bored or impatient |
| Looking at a clock or watch | Implies you want to move on to something else |
| Staring unblinkingly at the other person | Suggests aggression |
| Tapping your foot | Suggests nervousness or impatience |
| Sitting with crossed arms | Looks as if you are defending yourself against the other person's ideas |
| Sitting with crossed legs; sitting hunched | Looks as if you are trying to make yourself smaller, as if you lack confidence |
| Turning your chair slightly away from the other person | Implies lack of interest or (depending on other body language) lack of confidence |
| Reading papers at the same time the other person is talking to you | Implies lack of interest |
| Touching your face while talking | Implies timidity, especially if the hand is actually in front of the mouth |
| Rubbing your nose, looking away | Sometimes suggests lying |
| Scowling or frowning | Suggests disapproval |
| Avoiding eye contact | Suggests lack of interest or lack of confidence |
| Speaking slowly and deliberately, while the other person is speaking quickly | Suggests lack of self-awareness |
| Sitting back in your chair when the other person is sitting forward | Suggests lack of involvement |

## Creating rapport

### Matching

Rapport is about matching the other person, however fleetingly, as a way of showing them respect. Michael, for example, found that he was able to improve his interactions with his team by making some very simple changes in his behavior: pulling up a chair, sitting down at the desk of the person he was talking to, lowering his voice so that it was not so loud, and making sure that the pleasant smile on his face conveyed the nice guy he felt he really was.

This works even in some very extreme situations. For instance, imagine the following situations:

■ An angry person marches into your office and demands your attention.
■ A team member comes in to see you and is in tears.

What do you do? Before you say a word, you can use the techniques of establishing rapport to ensure that you have a fair chance of influencing the other person.

**THE ANGRY COLLEAGUE**
Get up from your desk immediately, keep your face friendly; but make sure that your own voice is also firm while you say, "I can see you're really angry."

**THE TEAM MEMBER WHO CRIES**
Immediately ask him or her to sit down with you; keep your voice quiet and soft.

### Match, don't copy

Of course this matching must be done with respect and without exaggeration. If people think you are deliberately copying them, it will have the opposite effect from the one you want.

When you have matched other people, you can then lead them – in other words, get them to follow you.

This takes a degree of focus and self-awareness. You have to know and control your own habits first. Then you can set up the conversation, so that the other person mirrors you for part of the time. If you are following them for the whole conversation, it can mean that they have all the control, whereas the ideal is for control to be shared.

People who are absolute experts in matching will claim that they can match the most subtle aspects of other people's body language: their breathing (rapid, shallow, deep) and even their facial color. But, for most of us, a basic level of competency, such as the one discussed below, will be sufficient.

**When you need to have an influencing conversation, here is a useful checklist:**

- Sit where you can see a clock without turning your head.
- Sit at a matching angle to the other person; never sit opposite them because it creates a confrontational impression.
- Choose furniture to facilitate the conversation – easy chairs and no tables are ideal.
- Concentrate on maintaining open body posture – hands palm up and open; uncrossed legs, arms, or feet.
- Remove anything you might "fiddle with" such as pens, or papers.
- Manage your voice – tone, volume and delivery – so that it matches the other person's. If he or she is speaking quickly, speed up your own speech; if he or she is speaking enthusiastically, keep your own voice sounding interested and passionate.
- Manage your eye contact. Too much will look aggressive. Too little will suggest lack of interest.

All this information can, of course, be used in the opposite way if you actually want to turn influencing into aggression. The writer, Gavin Kennedy, quotes one such example in his book *The New Negotiating Edge*. A group of social workers at war with their bosses insisted on having a meeting where there was a normal height table, with them on one side, bosses on the other. This was instead of the circular arrangement of easy chairs and coffee tables that social workers use for "difficult" meetings with clients. The social workers said they did not want any of that "manipulative stuff" getting in the way of a decent confrontation!

# Genuine listening

A colleague was recently running an event for a Buddhist monastery with a group of men whose whole way of life is concerned with attentive listening and respect for others. At one point, the Abbot reproachfully said, "There are several people here whose absence fills the room." In other words, they were physically present, but not actively listening.

After rapport, listening is probably the most powerful tool at your disposal as an influencer. Listening is one of the main ways we communicate the acceptance and respect that are an essential prerequisite for influencing someone else successfully. The two most important rules in influencing someone else effectively may be the most counter-intuitive:

- **PUT YOUR EFFORT INTO UNDERSTANDING THE OTHER PERSON FIRST.**
- **BE PREPARED TO BE INFLUENCED BEFORE YOU TRY TO INFUENCE THE OTHER PERSON.**

## Where do we go wrong?

Most of us do the opposite to both these rules. We try first to put our own points of view with varying degrees of vehemence. We also often start with a fixed position, whether we declare it or not. We see the task of influencing as bringing the other person around to our point of view, which often involves ignoring what they have to say.

Real listening means being able to listen without feeling the need to criticize, advise, argue, persuade or collude. It means genuinely accepting what the other person is expressing.

## There are many ways of communicating nonacceptance: Have you done any of these?

- **FALSE REASSURANCE**
  *This isn't a serious issue.*
- **TRIVIALIZING**
  *You don't want to worry about that.*
- **CLICHE**
  *Time heals anything.*
- **DISMISSING**
  *This idea is so silly, isn't it?*
- **INTERPRETING**
  *I think your main concern is with your reputation.*
- **DIAGNOSING TOO SOON**
  *I think the real problem here is the relationship with your boss.*

- **LABELING**
  *This is sexism, isn't it?*
- **PREACHING**
  *The right thing to do here is...*
- **BEING IMPATIENT**
  *What did you want to ask?*
  *Can we get on with that now?*
- **COLLUDING**
  *I think you're right; you have been victimized.*

## The second lever of influencing

To get around the traps listed opposite, you need to be able to use the second lever of influencing – genuine listening.

Real listening is very hard work. Most of us have developed the habit of half or even a quarter listening. We do pretend-listening: "Yes, I am listening, go on…" or, "I hear what you say," inevitably followed by BUT. No wonder it is so common to have people say, "But I told you that last week. You obviously weren't listening!"

Research into people acknowledged to be excellent negotiators has shown some interesting results. Such people listen about twice as often as they speak; and they use a number of techniques, such as summarizing, asking questions, and clarifying far more frequently than the average person. There are a number of reasons why this is an important advantage in a negotiating situation, which is after all, simply a more formal version of influencing:

- It allows you to get right inside the other person's mind so that you really know what he or she is thinking.
- It allows you to check out any assumptions you are making about his or her motives and concerns
- It gives you time to think and consider your next move.

- It demonstrates respect for the other person and his or her views.

Since listening is so useful, why is it that it is so difficult? Here is a list of barriers to effective listening.

### Barriers to effective listening
**Are any of these your problem?**
- I've heard all this before.
- What you're saying might be painful to hear.
- I know already that I disagree, so I'm getting my reply ready now.
- I've heard you say this before, and I wasn't interested then.
- I'm very busy now, so I'm just pretending to listen.
- My attention is wandering to something more interesting.
- If I show I'm interested, you might go on even longer; and I'm already bored.
- I hate the jargon you're using.
- This is much too theoretical for me.
- I find you frightening, so I want to get away now.
- I'm waiting impatiently for my turn in the conversation.

### No faking!

When I teach listening in my courses, many people say that, even in a practice with another person for five minutes or so, it is overwhelming to receive so much full attention. Real listening cannot be faked. To do it you really have to be what is called "fully present" for the other person. This means bringing your whole mind and body to the experience.

## Genuine listening

### How to do it

Your aim is empathy – a nonjudgmental state that aims to understand the other person. You want to know what he or she really thinks and feels. To empathize, you have to listen with exquisite attention.

### Stage 1
#### Listening for content

Give your whole attention to the other person. Banish your own views from your mind and concentrate on suspending your own judgement, especially in situations where you vehemently disagree with whatever views the other person is expressing.

### Stage 2
#### Listening for the other messages

Attentive listening means taking in not only the words people are using, but also the whole range of other signals they are sending. This will include:

- How they are sitting
- Their eye contact
- Facial expression and skin, including changes of color, or sweating
- The emotion in or behind the words
- What is left out
- The "underlying music" – the implied messages
- Tone and volume of voice

### Stage 3
#### Summarizing

When people say that genuine empathetic listening is "just a technique," I point out that the argument usually falls apart at this stage. Summarizing is the part of the conversation where in just a few words you sum up what you think you have heard. This is not the parrot-like "reflecting back" that some people have learned in management courses. It is a skillful summary that captures the essence of what the other person has said.

It works in the following way. Suppose the other person has spent five minutes telling you why she is unhappy in her job and would like to move on. She has described the long journey to work and the lack of promotion opportunities, as well as the competitive atmosphere in her team. Instead of doing what 99 percent of us would do and say, "I understand," the skilled influencer does something very different. He or she will then take about 30 seconds to say, "So, let me make sure I'm getting this right. You feel you would like to move on because the commute to work is taking nearly an hour, and that's really very tiring. Also, you don't feel you're really getting anywhere here, and you find the atmosphere on the team a bit too competitive for your liking. Is that how you see it?"

There are several things to notice about this technique:

- It does not contain any judgment or any of your views; you can give them later if necessary and appropriate.
- It ends with a question, so that the other person can correct you if you have it wrong.
- It is a genuine summary, not a long ramble through the same territory.
- It accurately conveys the other person's views.
- It implies the ultimate compliment to the other person: you have listened with scrupulous care and respect to what they have said – so scrupulously that you can summarize it accurately.
- For the time you are summarizing, you have control of the conversation, even though what you are reflecting is the other person's views. This can be particularly important with a talkative person. Summarizing gives you a legitimate reason to break into the conversation. This may be one of the few types of interruption that is never perceived as rude or dismissive.

These techniques work even if the other person uses them, too, because it is natural for us to respond positively when we hear our own views accurately and clearly summarized.

**Useful summarizing vocabulary**

- So let me try a summary here…
- I'm anxious to see whether I've really understood the points you're making…
- So, if I've got this right, your reasons are…
- Just to see where we are so far, you feel that there are three points here…

## Stage 4
### Summarizing the emotion

To do this takes even more skill because you have to be truly alert to every nuance in the conversation. You are noticing not only the content but also what has *not* been said.

In a conversation with a colleague that starts with a disagreement about how to approach a project and ends up as an angry confrontation over who gets to have his own way, you could try using these techniques. You might say, "Although I'm feeling angry myself, I'm going to try and summarize what your views are. You appear to think I never agree to do things your way or accept your suggestions on how the job might be done. You seem to be angry and very irritated with me. This is interpreting or judging – not summarizing. Have I got that right?"

## Genuine listening

In most such conversations, even those that are full of yelling and shouting, using this technique is the best and probably the only way of reaching peace. The other person invariably calms down, and, as long as you can remain calm yourself, you will both be able to resume a more normal kind of conversation.

### Stage 5
#### Testing your assumptions

Chris Argyris has written incisively about what he calls "left-hand and right-hand" thinking. Left-hand thinking is what we think but don't say. It contains our untested assumptions about the other person's motivation and thought processes. The right-hand side is what we actually do say. Here's an example: I have asked a secretary to do some typing for me. Argyris suggests that very often in a situation where there is some tension, we can swiftly go up what he calls the "Ladder of Inference," ending at a place that prevents influencing the other person successfully.

### WHAT I THOUGHT

I know he hasn't finished it; he's so slow.

If I'd given it to Milly, she'd have done it; she's much quicker.

Of course, this is such a boring job, just typing all day long, I don't know how anyone can stand it, but why he isn't faster, when all he does all day is type? Probably he's just wasting time.

I bet it'll be full of typos; he never reads things and can't be bothered to use spellcheck.

### WHAT I SAID

I: John, have you finished that typing yet?

John: No, I'm only about half way through it.

I: Oh, well, do your best.

John: I've got a lot to do this morning.

I: When you've finished that, I'll review it and then I'll explain what I'd like you to do next.

He's a hopeless PA

He's lazy

Typing's a boring job

He can't be bothered

He makes mistakes

He's slow

It is easy to go up a ladder of inference which is based on untested assumptions, as in the example above.

Successful influencing usually means that all the key assumptions will be tested on both sides, at some point, rather than leaving them unsaid. When you are stuck in a discussion, it is often worth mentally looking at your "left-hand column" to see what assumptions you and the other person are making. In this example, I have jumped from, "He's slow," to, "He's a hopeless administrative assistant," in one or two swift steps, instead of checking into John's actual situation.

## If I did, I might find that:

- He's slow because he has too many other things to do.
- He makes mistakes because he's never had proper typing training and doesn't know how to use spellcheck.
- He may be bothered, but he has picked up my disappointment and is feeling undermined.
- He doesn't find typing a boring job; he actually likes it.
- He's not lazy, just timid.
- With time and training, he could become a very good administrative assistant.

The technique here is to surface the other person's assumptions. You can only do this by making space in the conversation and asking him to tell you what his assumptions are.

**Useful phrases for testing assumptions:**
- **Can I just check what you really want here?**
- **Is your assumption that we can/can't do x or y?**
- **Would you mind telling me what your basic assumptions are here?**
- **I'm beginning to make some assumptions here about what you might want, but could I see whether I've clearly understood?**

# Questions

Skilled influencers ask many times more questions than unskilled ones. They also listen with a lot more care to the answers they get. Questions are another powerful "pull" lever.

Questioning does not mean interrogating. It does not mean putting people on the spot, where the assumption is that the person being questioned definitely has something to hide. It is not about asking loaded questions, either.

The kind of question you ask determines the response you will get.

*"Are you good at your job?"*

*"Yes."*

End of the conversation. This is a closed question because it can only be answered "yes" or "no" or with a few words. Here's another example:

*"Wouldn't you agree that it's a good idea to have regular team meetings?"*

*"Oh yes, of course."*

Here, too, there is nothing more to be said, because this is a leading question that expects agreement. The question is really a statement in disguise.

Skill in influencing requires skill in knowing what sorts of questions to ask and when to ask them.

## Open questions

Open questions are probably the most useful of all. They are particularly appropriate when your aim is to get the other person to talk and express an opinion, so that you can understand her clearly. This kind of question is linked closely to the skill of listening. As an influencer, you are more likely to be successful if you can draw people out (use "pull" techniques), than if you are busy talking, yourself.

Open questions encourage everyone to speak, because they cannot be answered "yes" or "no." Open questions usually begin "what," "where," "how," "when" or "tell me" (the most useful of all).

Imagine someone wants to know your views on the future of your organization:

**Closed and open questions:**

1. Do you think this organization has a future? (closed)
   What sort of future do you think this organization has? (open)

2. Should we merge with company x or stay as we are? (closed)
   What do you feel about a possible merger with company x? (open)

3. Wouldn't you agree that the Board has good ideas on future direction? (closed)
   Tell me, what do you think of the Board's ideas for the future? (open)

### A word about "why?"

"Why" is also an open question, but it is one to use with care:

- It can sound like an interrogation or accusation: "Why don't you like working in this office?"
- People may not know the answer. Sometimes the question beginning "why" is answered by "I don't know."

'What' is usually a better question. Instead of, "Why don't you like the office,"? try "What is it about the office that you don't like?"

Closed questions have their place. They are useful when you want to bring a particular conversation to an end or where you want to establish the facts.

- Did you get that report done?
- Are you able to go to the conference?
- So, can we agree that you will do that assignment by October 31?

Communication can also get fuzzy. We speak in generalizations, hoping that others will follow what we mean. Often, when you are hoping to influence someone, this fuzziness starts to get in the way; and your ability to influence is lost.

The art is to uncover the meaning by getting the other person to make his or her statements specific.

On the next page is a chart showing different types of fuzzy communication and suggestions for clarification.

## GENERALIZED NOUNS/ADJECTIVES

Fuzzy statement:

This department is unhappy.

Clarifying question:

*What is it, specifically, that's making people unhappy?*

In general, ask *"what"* questions.

## GENERALIZED VERBS

Fuzzy statement:

I hate the way he behaves in public.

Clarifying question:

*In what way do you hate the behavior specifically?* or,
*What is it about the behavior that you hate?*

In general, ask *"what"* or *"how"* questions

## IMPLIED RULES: SHOULDS, SHOULDN'TS, MUSTS

Fuzzy statements:

She should consult us more.

Clarifying questions:

*What would happen (or stop happening) if she did consult us more?*

In general, bring the assumptions behind the rule to the surface.

## GENERALIZATIONS: ALL, ALWAYS, EVERYONE, NEVER, EVERY

Fuzzy statement:

He always shows up late for meetings

Clarifying question:

*Always? Are there ever any exceptions?*

In general, challenge the generalization; ask for exceptions.

## COMPARISONS: BETTER, WORSE, EASIER, HARDER, BIGGER, SMALLER

Fuzzy statement:

Other people are better mangers than he is.

Clarifying question:

*Better at what? Better in what ways, specifically?*

In general, make the implied comparison explicit.

## IMPLIED HELPLESSNESS

Fuzzy statement:

I don't know whether to leave my present job.

Clarifying question:

*What would help you decide?* or, *What would persuade you to stay (or go)?*

In general, ask *"what"* questions

## PROBLEM ORIENTATION

Fuzzy statement:

There's so much stress and tension here.

Clarifying question:

*If the stress disappeared, what would replace it?*

In general, ask reframing or solution-orientated questions.

## Questions to ask

Questioning combined with real rapport, careful listening, and summarizing is by far the best alternative to the clumsy influencing technique of attempting to offer advice. There are certain $64,000 questions. They are more or less guaranteed to get people talking and to get them talking in a way that magically enables them to answer their own questions with wise advice. Sounds improbable? Give it a try. Think about a problem that is really bothering you. Go through the list of questions below. Read them aloud, and say your answers aloud; don't just think them.

### The $64,000 questions:

1 What's the issue here – the presenting problem?
2 Who and what is involved?
3 On a scale of 1-10, how important is this problem? (If it only counts as a two or three then you can give up at this point!)
4 How much energy are you prepared to put into solving the problem?
5 What have you already tried in the way of resolving it?
6 In an ideal world, what would be the solution to the problem? What would be happening? How would you know the problem had been solved?
7 What's standing in the way of the problem being solved now?
8 What have you contributed to the problem?
9 When you've had a problem like this before and solved it successfully, what did you do?
10 Who and what else is helping you move towards the ideal outcome?
11 If you imagine yourself at your most resourceful, what would you say to yourself about how to resolve this issue?
12 What must happen to make your advice a reality?
13 Who can help you turn the advice into reality?

## An advanced skill

When you have experienced the power of these questions for yourself, try them with other people. They are especially useful in situations where other people turn to you for advice. Listening with empathy, not offering an opinion, summarizing carefully, and asking these questions are among one of the most certain ways of helping people to help themselves. Paradoxically, this is one of the effective influencer's most advanced skills and certainly all managers' duty where their teams are concerned.

# 5

## The "push" skills of influencing
## Assertiveness
## Giving feedback

**Aggression and passivity**

**Saying "no"**

**The dangers of criticism**

# Assertiveness: asking for what you want

Recent research and thinking has suggested that, although we tend to think of ourselves as a sophisticated species, we may be deluding ourselves. These researchers point out that, because there has been no major climatic or other environmental challenge to the human species, essentially, we are the same psychologically as we were when we emerged from the Savannah in Africa 200,000 years ago.

As Professor Nigel Nicholson put it in his article on this subject in the *Harvard Business Review*, "You can take man out of the Stone Age, but you can't take the Stone Age out of man." Much of our behavior may be "hard-wired" to instinctively protect us in the same way that was necessary when life was short, fragile, and dangerous.

If true, perhaps this explains why so many of our responses to danger fall into two simple categories: fight or flight. Our typical experiences as children may also contribute to this pattern. As children, we learn that adults have the power to make us miserable through constantly dictating how we should behave. We learn that:

- Children should be seen and not heard.
- If you answer back too loudly and too often you will get punished.

- You should do what you are told.
- Adults know best.
- It is naughty to be selfish.

The effect of these messages can be destructive. Two responses can develop:

- **Aggression:** fighting back, being "strong" by demanding, yelling, boasting, fighting, name calling, and insisting on getting what you want through forcefulness, regardless of what others may need. Here, we keep danger at bay by being constantly on the alert, trying to control others through conscious or unconscious intimidation.
- **Passivity:** running away (flight), always putting others' needs first, giving in, feeling like a perpetual loser, and being timid. Here, we have absorbed the message from childhood that we are "bad." We try to keep badness hidden by being consciously or unconsciously "good." This means repressing all our own wishes because, that way, we will never provoke the anger in others that frightened us so much as children.

These two responses may be our most instinctive human responses. To find a third way does not come easily, and most of us have to learn it consciously. It is the skill of assertiveness.

## Is aggression your pattern?

| Do you: | Yes | No |
|---|---|---|
| Interrupt people often? | | |
| Get impatient when you can't have your own way? | | |
| Get angry quickly? | | |
| Complain quickly when something is not up to your expectations? | | |
| Create situations where you can feel in control? | | |

## Or is passivity more your style?

| Do you: | Yes | No |
|---|---|---|
| Find it difficult to complain? | | |
| Often find yourself apologizing? | | |
| Find it difficult to ask for what you want? | | |
| Often tell yourself you shouldn't make a fuss? | | |
| Want to be perfect in other people's eyes? | | |

## Assertiveness: asking for what you want

### Are you passive or aggressive?

Possibly, you flit between the two. Neither aggressive nor passive behavior is likely to get you what you want. As influencing tactics they are hopeless:

■ **Aggressive** people create further aggression. In not noticing or caring about the impact of their behavior, they hurt others. Their competitiveness often leads to health problems caused by trying too hard, too much of the time.

Aggression is a response to the frustration of not feeling in control and is one of the ways we try to keep the demons of helplessness away.

■ **Passive** people also feel anger, but the anger has gone to sleep and emerges disguised as anxiety about whether or not they are liked. Sometimes, the passive person seeks to care for others. By caring for others, the passive person hopes to be taken care of in return. Passive people do not get what they want because no one knows what they want. Indeed, they often do not know themselves. They may feel that they are exploited because they find it so difficult to say "no." Often the price to be paid for passive behavior is attacks of anxiety and depression.

The passive person is concerned with the "If Onlys" of the Circle of Concern (page 22): "If only I had a partner who really respected me," … "If only my boss didn't bully me," … "If only I worked in an organization where people were valued."

The good news is that assertiveness is a genuine middle path between the brutal selfishness of the aggressive person and the hidden anger of the passive one.

### What is assertiveness?

Assertiveness is about balancing your needs with the needs of other people. It is about demonstrating respect for others as well as self-respect. As an assertive person you can:

■ Say no without causing offence.
■ Ask for what you want without stepping on others.
■ Ask for what you need without fear of being derided or criticized.
■ Describe your feelings to others without embarrassment.
■ Complain without humiliating the other person.
■ Ask for your rights to be respected while staying calm and respectful.
■ Remain in control even in difficult situations.

Being assertive means accepting yourself for who you are. It means you know you're not perfect, so you can accept feedback. It means you cannot be hurt by people unless you grant them this right.

## Authority figures

Assertiveness means that you see authority figures in their proper roles as imperfect human beings just like you. You know that even if you are "good," no one will look after you and protect you – not your boss, your partner, the government, or anyone else – because only you can look after yourself.

Assertiveness is not just a fancier and more acceptable name for aggression.

Assertiveness means you know you have rights, but with those rights goes the responsibility to treat others in the same way you expect to be treated – with courtesy and dignity. It also means that you accept accountability for your own actions. If you complain about the service in a shop, you are exerting your right to complain, but you must also be accountable for the response that your complaint creates.

## The bill of rights and responsibilities

Assertiveness is often associated with a number of basic human rights, but each one has its own corresponding responsibility (see below):

| You have the right to | And responsibility for |
| --- | --- |
| Be heard. | Making sure that you hear others |
| Change your mind. | Encouraging others to rethink and reconsider |
| Choose. | Ensuring that others' choices are respected |
| Make mistakes. | Seeing that other people view mistakes as opportunities to learn |
| Say no. | Encouraging others to come to their own conclusions and to disagree with you if they wish |
| Ask for what you want. | Respecting that other people's needs may be different from yours |

## Assertiveness: asking for what you want

### The skills of assertiveness

#### Assertive body language

How you hold yourself conveys your self-respect. The key features are:

- Relaxed but upright posture; spine kept in a straight line but not rigid; head in the middle of your body, not cocked to one side or bent forward, both of which look apologetic
- Eye contact maintained with the other person; not staring (aggressive); or avoided (passive)
- Smiling, relaxed facial muscles
- Relaxed hands and arms; not wringing your hands nervously (passive) or balled fists (aggressive). Never cross your arms when you are trying to look assertive; it suggests defensiveness
- Gestures under control: no fidgeting with hair, pens, sleeves, rings, belts, pockets, all of which look apologetic and passive
- Avoid aggressive gestures, such as finger-jabbing, arm-waving, and getting so close to people that you seem to be invading their personal space
- Steady, calm voice; not too loud, not too soft

### Using assertive language

Assertive language is straightforward and respectful – to yourself and to the other person. The most important word you can use is "I":

*I want you to do…*
*I'd like you to…*
*I need you to…*

Stating a need is particularly powerful because no one else can tell you that you do not have it.

Avoid being tentative or apologetic:

*I'd sort of like you to…*
*Perhaps it might be a good idea, when you've got time, of course, to…*
*I'm sorry to ask you this, but…*

### Making requests

It is surprising how difficult it can feel to make requests, even in such straightforward situations as asking a team member to complete a piece of work. An inner, critical voice can be saying:

- He's probably too busy, and his time matters more than mine.
- I expect he'll get around to it on his own if I just wait.
- He might say "no," and then I'd feel silly.

If you find yourself hesitating in these situations, remind yourself of two things. First, you have the right to make requests, and it is impossible to extend your range of influence unless you do. Recognizing this is very important.

Secondly, what's the worst thing that could happen? Probably the worst that could happen is that the other person says "no." Would that really be a disaster?

## Here is a simple formula for making requests:

### 1. Use the person's name

The American writer, Dale Carnegie, the author of the first big bestseller on influencing, *How to Win Friends and Influence People*, first published more than sixty years ago, made the point that a person's name is, to them, the most important sound in the world.

And he was right. I worked once as coach to a senior manager who was in terrible trouble with his human relationships. When I shadowed him for a day – that is, just discreetly sat in on his meetings and walked around his unit with him – I saw one reason why immediately. He not only never addressed people by name, he didn't even know most people's names. He barked orders at them and always addressed them as "you." He did not disguise the fact that he did not know any of their names and, in fact, could not really be bothered to learn them at all.

Contrast this with the boss of a large charity who knows the names of every single one of the people working at headquarters and remembers and uses the names of the all people working in the shops run by the charity.

If you don't use people's names when you address them, they assume they are anonymous to you. And, if they are anonymous to you, why should they do what you want?

### 2. State your request in a straightforward manner, using the word "I."

Don't wander around the issue, wrapping it up with ifs and buts or attributing the request to others. Instead, be direct: "Anne, I'd like you to stand in for Donna today please."

*Or*

"Phil, I need you to work at Reception today please."

Unassertive versions of the same requests would be:

## Assertiveness: asking for what you want

"I'm really sorry to interrupt you because I know how busy you are, but you're needed to stand in for Donna today." This is the passive version, as it apologizes unnecessarily and attributes the request to unnamed forces.

*Or*

"Get yourself down to reception now!" (This is the aggressive version, probably accompanied by finger-jabbing).

### 3. Explain why

"Anne, I'd like you to stand in for Donna today, please. The reason is that Donna's just called in sick and we've got a real rush of work that has to be completed by today, so it's going to cause huge problems if we don't get it done."

"Phil, I need you to work at reception today please. We're expecting a steady stream of clients and it gives a really poor impression if there's no one at Reception to open the door for them, make them coffee and so on."

### 4. Invite their comments and solutions

Having made your request, you can then ask for their views – for instance on how it should be implemented, or on the implications for them. Here, useful phrases are, "How does that strike you?" or, "How should we organize things?"

### 5. Ask what resources are needed to make the request happen

People may be willing to carry out what you wish, but they may not have the time, budget or knowledge to do what you want. If so, you need to discuss it.

### 6. Agree the timescale

If you have asked Anne to stand in for Donna, you will need to say for how long. Again, the inner, unassertive voice may dread having to ask an already busy person to do something else. But if you don't agree a timescale, you will have left out one of the most important parts of the agreement.

## The broken record technique

This technique uses the metaphor of a broken record, when the same phrases are endlessly repeated.

It is a technique to use with care because it can seem crude, but in the right situation it can have dramatic effect. A few years ago, my husband, Alan, and I were travelling back from Norway. We arrived at Oslo airport late one afternoon to find that the carrier had over-booked the flight, there were no other planes to London with any carrier that day and we both had important meetings in London the next morning. The famed SAS customer care seemed to be in disarray and we were met with what seemed like total indifference.

After asking to see a senior manager, the conversation went like this:

**Alan: We need to be in London tonight because we have meetings tomorrow morning, so you must find us a flight somehow – it's your mistake anyway.**

SAS: We haven't got any seats – I'm sorry, there's nothing we can do. But we'll pay for a hotel and you can be on the first flight to London tomorrow morning.

**Alan: I can see your problem, but our problem is that we need to be in London by tomorrow morning, so we need you to find a way around this somehow.**

SAS: The plane is full and there aren't any other flights to London today.

**Alan: Yes, but our problem is that we need to be in London in the morning, so we must get to London tonight.**

SAS: I'll see if I can book you on a flight to Copenhagen and from there to London.

And this is what happened. So the broken record technique is a simple one. You briefly acknowledge what the other person has said, but go on asking for what you want, regardless of excuses.

# Assertiveness at meetings

If you are running meetings yourself, make sure that you do so in a way that makes it easy for others to be assertive:
■ Use round or hexagonal tables; they are better than square or rectangular ones.
■ Remove any spare chairs.
■ Close all the spaces between people.
■ Encourage the more silent people to join in by glancing in their direction from time to time.
■ Use communication skills to curb the over-talkative.

When I first started working as a coach to people in organizations, particularly if they were young, I was surprised by how many of them dreaded speaking at meetings. Now, I am used to it. "Help me get around this problem" is one of the most common requests my clients make. They describe feeling tongue-tied and embarrassed at the kinds of things they say when they do speak; or may feel that other people have said exactly what they would have said, if only they had found the courage to speak up first.

All the advice in this section applies to meetings, but there are some special tips you should bear in mind.

■ The most important is to make sure you speak in the first five minutes of the meeting. Patterns of interaction get set remarkably quickly. The longer you say nothing, the more likely it is that people will assume you have nothing to say. Saying something also helps get over the initial nervousness that many people feel in meeting situations.

■ Think about where you sit. If you want to get into the discussion, it is best to sit directly opposite the meeting leader, since you are right in his or her line of sight. The worst place is two chairs down from the leader, on the same side of the table.

■ Watch your body language. If you sit slumped or push your chair away it is going to be much harder to be taken seriously when you do want to make a statement.

■ Speak up, keep your voice strong.

■ Smile.

■ Engage everyone at the meeting with eye contact. Don't do what a lot of people do, which is address all their remarks to the chair.

■ Prepare carefully. If there are pre-meeting papers, make sure you read them. Many people do not bother. If you have bothered, you will have a huge advantage.

■ Speak up if you disagree. Ask whether others feel the same. Often you will find that others disagree, too, but have not found the courage to say so. If you find you are alone in your views, then accept it graciously.

■ Use summarizing techniques to help the chair clarify the discussion, especially where there is conflict.

■ Fulfill any commitments you agree to take on at the meeting.

■ Beware of any "I'm-not-interested" behavior: doodling, bringing your in-box with you to read during the boring parts, rushing out to make phone calls, leaving your cellphone switched on so that it could ring, arriving late, and leaving early.

# Saying "no"

Having to say "no" gets to the heart of why some people find it difficult to be assertive. Typical "no" situations might be:

- Refusing a team member's request to go on vacation at a particular date
- Saying no to a request for an increase in salary
- Telling a partner that you'd rather stay in and watch TV than go out
- Telling a door-to-door salesman you do not want any of his dish cloths or oven mits.

Do any of these thoughts occur to you when you have to say "no"?

- The other person may dislike me for it.
- I'll be rejected if I don't go along with it.
- The other person may get angry, and I wouldn't know what to do.
- The other person may get upset and cry. What then?
- It may look selfish or rude.

If you can't say "no" when it is perfectly legitimate to do so, you run the risk of being exploited by others. Ultimately, you may become so fed up with being considered a doormat that you have occasional outbursts, where you resort to aggressiveness and all your anger erupts. Again, there is a simple formula format to follow. These are the steps to take:

- Acknowledge the person's right to make the request. For example, "I can understand why you want to go out tonight because you've been working so hard. You need a bit of light relief."
- Say "no" straightforwardly: "I don't want to go out. I'd rather stay here."
- Explain your feelings; then give your reasons. For example, "I feel really tired, and I've had a really difficult day. I just don't have the energy to get changed and drive to the restaurant. The idea of staying here and just "veging" in front of the TV appeals to me much more."
- Suggest an alternative. This is important because it shows that you are trying to meet the other person's needs as well as your own. For example, "I wonder if we could go out tomorrow instead; or maybe x or y would like to go with you, if you really prefer to go tonight?"

This formula works, even with senior people in your organization. If your boss asks you to take on a project; but you are already very busy, you might say, "I can see how important this work is, but I can't take it on now. I'm already over-extended. My suggestion would be to postpone the start of the project. If it could wait for three days, I would take it on with pleasure. How does that sound to you?"

# Feedback

**A**t some point, successful influencing will always involve the "push" skill of giving feedback. Ask yourself whether you have been in these situations recently:

- **Working with a team member whose performance has fallen below the acceptable standard**
- **Living with a partner, son, daughter or parent whose behavior has persistently annoyed you**
- **Being on the receiving end of poor service from a garage, restaurant, shop, or other service-provider**

In such situations you have a number of choices for action. Which one do you typically choose?

1. Ignore it and hope it goes away on its own
2. Shout, scream, lose your temper, say you rue the day you were ever involved with such incompetents
3. Apologize
4. Calmly give feedback on the behavior

Number 4 is the only one that is at all likely to have any permanent impact. Feedback is a word much bandied about, but it is also much abused and misunderstood. Let's be clear what it is.

## Feedback is not the same as criticism

For instance, let's say that you are working with a new administrative assistant. She is late several times over a period of a few weeks, despite your asking her several times to be ready for work by nine o' clock each day.

If you criticize her, you might say something like this:

*"For heaven's sake! You're late again. Your time-management is terrible. This is really irresponsible. I can't stand it. Unless you get your act together you'll have to go! Everyone here thinks you're hopeless!"*

Being on the receiving end of criticism is devastating. In many years of working with people on how to give feedback, I always collect their comments on what it has felt like to be the focus of criticism. It's always the same, regardless of people's age, seniority, or experience.

Some examples of their experiences have included:

- He made me feel like a stupid, two-year-old child.
- I felt really frightened. I wondered what he was going to do next.
- I wanted revenge – immediately!
- I answered back; I didn't care about the consequences at all.
- I thought, "You can wave goodbye to any thought of loyalty whatsoever!"

## Feedback mode

If the same conversation happens in feedback mode, it is very different. It might go, in a calm and reasonable tone, like this:

*"I noticed you didn't get into the office until 9:30 again this morning. And there were two days last week when you got here at 9:45 and 9:55. We did agree that we would all be starting at 9.00. The fact that you weren't here caused a lot of difficulty. The phones were ringing, and we lost calls. I'd like you to be sure of being here at 9:00 in future, but let's hear your side. What was the reason that you were late on those days?"*

The effect of these two styles is very different. The first brings out all the defensive and aggressive reactions described above because it contains hurtful generalization: *terrible time-management, irresponsibility, everyone thinks...* With the second, it is impossible to ignore the specific detail, and it is much less easy to wriggle away with excuses or counterattacks.

Also, the fact that the person has been asked for his or her view allows for the possibility that there is some reasonable explanation. The table sums up the differences between the two modes:

| FEEDBACK | CRITICISM |
|---|---|
| Meant to improve performance in a positive way | A way of unloading anger |
| Calm | Angry |
| Tough on the issues | Tough on the person |
| Specific: quotes detailed evidence, gives facts, describes the person's actual behavior | Vague and gives opinions: makes generalizations. Look out for words like always, never |
| Future focus: "What I'd like to see you do in future is..." | Past focus |
| Looks for solutions | Looks for scapegoat |
| Looks for underlying causes | The last person in the chain gets the blame |
| Two way | One way |
| Person giving the feedback owns their opinion, says "I think..." | Person defining the feedback attributes opinions to others: they or we think so and so |

## Feedback

### Criticism vs. feedback

The key difference between the two is that feedback describes fact; criticism gives an opinion. "Your time-management is terrible" is an opinion. "You didn't get here until 9:45" is fact.

When you want to make some positive comment on a person's work, there's also a difference between appreciation and feedback. Here, it is a difference of degree.

Let's suppose that, again, you are working with an administrative assistant. You want to show her you have noticed that she has stayed late and done good work: "Thanks for staying late. I really appreciate the good work you've done here."

Now this is pleasant to hear and a lot better than not being thanked at all. However, it does not have the profoundly lasting and weighty effect of something like this:

"Thanks so much for staying late. I know it was a sacrifice because it's a pain

## GIVING EFFECTIVE FEEDBACK - HOW TO DO IT

■ Put the emphasis on the positive: give positive and focused feedback all the time. "Catch them doing something right." Do this about ten times more often than you think is natural. For most of us, our appetite for good news about ourselves is literally unlimited. Being given many short, focused pieces of feedback has much more impact than the occasional long one.

■ Do it immediately. This nips "bad habits" in the bud and gets around the "Why didn't you tell me before?" problem.

■ Focus on specifics, describe behavior, cite facts. For example, "The way you managed that job by doing x or y was perfect because you ..."

■ Describe the impact of behavior.
   Examples: "I was glad you let me know so early about the changes in the plan because, as a result, I was able to let x or y know in ample time."
   "The fact that you were late caused all of us significant inconvenience."

having to stay late, but flexible hours are all part of the way we work here. Staying and finishing that document meant that I was able to present it confidently this morning. I noticed you'd used 14-point type as well. That was great because I could read it at a glance at the meeting."

This sends a much more important message about what you expect and will reward. You do want flexibility; you do want initiative; it was a tremendous help to you to have the document in a format you could readily use. That person will know in future that this is the behavior you want to see.

Without feedback, an employee has no idea whether his or her performance is good or bad and how it could improve. As a manager, giving skilfull feedback is one of the simplest ways to influence people. Managers worry about how to reward people when there is often no budget for bonuses. Feedback costs nothing and has as lasting an impact as extra money.

## GIVING EFFECTIVE FEEDBACK – HOW TO DO IT

■ Do it when you are calm. Feedback is meant to be helpful.
Specifically suggest what you would prefer to see (if you have to give negative feedback) and offer useful suggestions for preventing similar mistakes in future. Example: "That first sentence in your report had too much information in it for people to take in. I suggest, instead, that you redo with half the content, so that people can absorb the main points first."

■ Follow up quickly with more feedback when you see improvements.

■ Give negative feedback in private; positive feedback can sometimes be given in public, depending on the circumstances.

■ Always ask how the person assesses him/herself.

■ Involve the other person fully in finding causes and solutions.

■ Ask for feedback on your own performance as a manager. If there is a problem performer, be certain in your own mind that you have considered the possibility that the problem is with you and not with the other person.

## Feedback

### Caveats

There are two overall caveats. The first is that you cannot give negative feedback if the other person cannot accept that there is a problem. As a boss myself, I once had a chronically poor performer on my team. Unfortunately, she simply could not accept or learn from the frequent – and I hope skillfully-offered – feedback she was given. Protesting bitterly, and to the end, that no one had ever mentioned these things before, she had to leave. Her inability to accept that there was a problem became the problem.

Second there is no point in giving people feedback about things they cannot change. If you gave me feedback about the remnants of my Welsh accent, I would have to say that there is nothing I can do about it, even in the unlikely event that I would want to. Similarly, it would be pointless to give a person of 5' 5" feedback about being too short to be a dancer. Saying that someone is too short would be a reason for not being able to become a professional dancer, but it is not feedback because there is nothing the person can do about it.

### Being open to influence: receiving feedback

To give feedback, you have to know how to receive it. Asking for feedback is one of the main ways you can demonstrate openness to other people's influence. Paradoxically, it is also one of the prime ways you can be an effective influencer yourself. You may get all kinds of feedback, most of it probably not very adeptly given. You may want to reject other people's feedback. For instance:

- You may not respect them or care what they think.
- It may not be clear what they mean. Many people are cautious about the response they may get and may couch their feedback in impossibly convoluted phrases.
- You may know they are just plain wrong.
- You may think they are right, but there is actually nothing you can do to change your behavior.

When people offer you feedback, they may be uncertain how you will receive it, or they may just not know how to do it properly because they have never had any training. So the feedback may take any of these forms:

- Apparent attack (criticism): "You're awful at giving presentations."
- Apparent compliment: "You're brilliant at giving presentations."
- Vague hints: "You're a bit hard to understand at times."

**Don't: get angry, defensive or self-justifying**
**Don't: immediately confess "guilt"**
**Much better tactics are to follow the format below.**

### Useful steps in receiving feedback

1. Repeat and summarize the feedback (review the section on summarizing). "So, you mean I talk too fast and use too much jargon?" This shows that you have understood and gives the other person the chance to correct you.

2. Ask for evidence. "When you say I talk too fast, can you give me a specific example?" "When you say I'm "brilliant at giving presentations," what do you mean exactly. Can you give me an example of something that worked especially well for you?"

3. Ask for ideas on how you could improve. "Could you tell me how you think I ought to say it?"

4. Give your side of things. "The reason I was so late giving the presentation was that I got caught in a bomb scare at the station, and there were no trains. I called the office, but your voice mail wasn't on."

5. Consider the other person's view.

6. Negotiate; agree on what should be done.

### Advantages of this method

Receiving feedback this way has a number of advantages, especially when it is feedback you have asked for.

Firstly, you will more than likely get some pleasant surprises. Second, it demonstrates that you really want to hear what other people think, even if you will also form your own view about how to respond to what they say. Next, there may be aspects of your behavior that really annoy or upset others. If so, you need to hear about them so that you can decide what to do.

Finally, and most important, it shows that you have the courage to stay open to what others think, allowing the possibility that they can influence you. This is one of the main characteristics of people who are good at influencing others because, when the time comes to say what you think, they are in a much more receptive frame of mind.

# 6

**Additional skills**
**Dealing with an impasse**
**Creating common ground**
**The wider scene**

**Acknowledging the blocks**

**Networking, influencing upwards, values**

**Action planning**

# Dealing with an impasse

Sometimes, in spite of all the techniques described so far, you reach an impasse. You have tried listening and summarizing (page 42); you have asked for what you want (page 54); but what you want and what the other person wants remain stubbornly at odds. There are a number of techniques you can try.

## No deal

First, consider the possibility that a deal is unlikely. When I was trying to sell my car a few years ago, I was approached by a friend. He offered me 20 percent less than the price I had hoped to get. The negotiation was very courteous on both sides. We both listened carefully and we both wanted to close the deal.

But I did not want to compromise on my target price, as I knew my car was worth what I was asking. And he could not increase his offer. I was prepared to go to the trouble of advertizing my car again, and he was prepared to go to the trouble of finding another car to buy. Here we had a no-deal situation. We shook hands, and that was that. This left the relationship intact with no hard feelings on either side.

## Draw attention to the impasse

Ninety-nine percent of the time we do not express what is wrong. Embarrassment or annoyance prevents it. When this happens there are often a number of undesirable consequences. You may get drawn into an agreement that you do not feel is right for the sake of keeping the peace. Both sides may know that the agreement cannot stick but hope for the best against their better judgement. Alternatively, tempers get frayed as each side presses for what it wants, not listening to the other.

If you reach an impasse, bring it into the open by saying something like, "We seem to have gotten stuck here. Let's see if we can find a way out of it."

By drawing attention to the process you take the initiative and demonstrate your commitment to finding a solution. It is also a powerful tactic to suggest that you and the other person work on how to break out of the impasse, rather than going around the same arguments over and over again.

## Identify the areas of agreement

Most of the time this does not happen. What happens instead is the opposite. We identify the areas of disagreement. Mediators who work with divorcing couples have often used this to great effect. Each partner may be consumed with dislike and even hatred for the other, but both love their children. Identifying that the common ground between the partners lies in the happiness of their children has often been the starting point for many a new agreement.

I worked with a team recently that was apparently divided by rampant conflict. Two people on the team were bitter that they had not been promoted; three others were engaged in harsh disputes about the boundaries of their jobs, each accusing the others of getting into their territory. It would have been easy to believe that the conflicts were all-consuming. But in discussion, the team agreed that it had total consensus about a new strategic direction and that this was much more important than the issues dividing them. The other issues were quietly resolved within a few weeks.

## Useful questions here:

*"Where do we agree?"*
*"Where do we disagree?"*
*"Can we identify the common ground?"*
*"What do we both agree on?"*
*Ask the "What would need to happen?" question.*
The latter is an awesomely powerful question. It puts some of the responsibility for finding a solution back on the other person.

Some examples:

| SITUATION | QUESTION |
|---|---|
| A team member has just announced her resignation. You want her to stay. | What has to happen to persuade you to stay? |
| A supplier is refusing to give you a discount. | What has to happen for us to be able to get a discount? |
| Your boss will not agree to letting you go to a training course. | What would I need to do to persuade you that this is a good idea? |

## Dealing with an impasse

### Recheck your assumptions – and theirs

Often when stuck, it is useful to revisit assumptions, by saying something like:

*"My assumption here is that what we're doing is… And your assumption seems to be that… Is that right?"*

This is particularly useful when feelings are running high. I was present recently at a heated discussion between a father and his teenage daughter. The daughter wanted to go to a club, coming home late by herself; and the father wanted the daughter to be home by midnight, picked up in the family car. The discussion was getting to the inflammatory level, (You think I'm still a little girl/ And you think you're an adult when you're still very young) when the father remembered that he had been trained in the techniques described here. He said, *"My basic assumption here is that it is too dangerous for you to come home on your own after midnight, and I need to know that you're safe. I also think you might want to get together with some boy you've never met before. Is that right?"*

She replied, *"I agree that you'd be worried, but the club doesn't start till 11.00, and no one goes home till at least 2.00. I'd look terrible leaving at midnight, especially if you picked me up."*

The discussion then became more open. The daughter was able to admit to being not quite so adventurous as she had claimed, and a cab, properly booked in advance for 1:30 a.m., was a compromise that was satisfactory to both sides.

### Talk about your feelings

Like many of these tactics, this one may seem counterintuitive. But it works. Instead of assuming that you have to remain in neutral throughout a discussion, it is actually much more effective to expose your feelings. If you are feeling angry and let down, say so; and ask what the other person is feeling. Talk candidly, too, about your own emotions, rather than speculating about the motivation of the other person.

For instance, in a negotiation over the price of goods from a supplier, you could say, *"When we failed to reach agreement on the price last night, I really did feel very disappointed. I wondered if it was something about the way I'd contributed to the conversation. I really hope that today we can find a solution."*

This is a whole lot better than thinking to yourself or, even worse, saying to the supplier, *"You seem to be out to get every penny you can out of my department."*

I saw this used to great effect by a manager who had reached an impasse with a boss on the subject of their working relationship. The boss had a flamboyant and demanding style, which often made him difficult to work with; but he couldn't see how this made life difficult for others. The younger manager ended the impasse by saying, *"David, I'm finding this discussion very frustrating. I'm disappointed that I haven't been able to get you to see how I feel, and I'm dreading going away again today feeling like I have so many times before."*

This was enough to break the tenor of the conversation.

## Name the blocks

A similar tactic is to name the obstacles. It is useful when the other person persistently creates the same kind of impasse. Types of resistance might be:

■ I don't have time to talk to you now.

■ It's someone else's fault.

■ Moralizing or intellectualizing: "This is an example of the double helix effect in this organization isn't it?"

Deal with this by naming the block. For instance:

Other tactics that can be used as a way of resisting someone can include:
■ **Being angry**
■ **Distracting you by going off on a tangent**
■ **Crying**
■ **Immediately confessing 'guilt', or saying 'sorry', before you have even had time to finish your sentence.**

| THE OTHER PERSON SAYS/DOES | YOU SAY |
|---|---|
| Rushes off – no time to talk | I notice that whenever I try to raise this subject, you tell me you don't have time. |
| It's someone else's fault | When we talk about this, I've noticed that you suggest it's not your responsibility, but someone else's. |
| Intellectualizing | I see that you're giving it a fancy label, but can we get back to the subject here? |

## Dealing with an impasse

### Reassure the other person of your sincerity in wanting to find a solution.

This is a very simple idea; but, again, it is easy to lose sight of it in the emotion of reaching an impasse. Saying to the other person, "I really do want us to find a solution that will keep us both happy" is a powerful lever. It reminds both of you that this really is what you want and can often work magically in taking the heat out of a difficult situation.

### Reaffirm your respect for the other side.

Similarly, this is also a strong card to play. It must be offered authentically. It works because it conveys, "We may have differences of opinion, but I still respect you as a person."

### Ask for a break to reconsider.

When feelings are running high, it can be useful to suggest a break to reconsider the whole thing. Opening or closing a window, having some coffee, taking a walk, or even sleeping on it, often brings a new sense of perspective.

### Ask what information might help if it were available.

This can be useful because it can save face. Use phrases such as:
- What don't we know here that would help if we did know it?
- What information is missing? How could we find out?

### Suggest a pilot project.

If the full-scale version is not possible, it is sometimes helpful to suggest a small project that can test your ideas. Providing a face-saving way out for all concerned is useful, because it creates time to think and allows for a genuine piece of road-testing for whatever ideas are under debate.

### Expose the difficulties rather than smoothe them over.

Skilled influencers do this even when, by doing so, they can appear to be losing the argument, which would seem foolish. However, it is usually better to expose difficulties early on than to try to patch them up later. If neglected, the areas of disagreement are likely to have grown and be even harder to sort out. Ignoring the awkward issues makes it more likely that your proposals will never be implemented.

## Traps in dealing with an impasse

Dealing with an impasse is possibly the most demanding situation of all where influencing is concerned. You need to be alert to a number of traps:

### Trap 1. Wanting to crawl away, because the other person has "won"

Wanting to retreat may be understandable, especially if you have been dealing with a bully. However, remember that you have the right to be treated with respect. A bully should be confronted, as this tactic is the only one he or she will understand.

Try the tactic described on page 72 and talk about your feelings. Say something like, "I have felt very uncomfortable during this discussion. It has made me feel bullied. I'm sure that wasn't your intention, but it's difficult to think clearly when, for instance, you raise your voice at me. I'd like us to have a calmer, more even-handed discussion. Do you think that is going to be possible?"

### Trap 2. Shouting and finger-pointing

Here, you will be encouraging the other person to match you – in the worst possible way. It may give you a temporary thrill to shout, but it is unlikely to help you reach agreement because it says, "I can shout louder; therefore you have got to do what I say." This behavior is unlikely to lead to a lasting agreement, though it may lead to temporary compliance. Try all the pull techniques instead.

### Trap 3. Making threats

Threats do not work for the same reason as Trap 2. They invite the other person to make a counterthreat. You, in turn, will be encouraged to make an even bigger threat, and eventually, neither party can back down without losing face. Wars start this way; and, in the end, both sides always have to sit down and negotiate.

### Trap 4. Taking a vote

Although a vote may seem like a "democratic" way to resolve the problem in the short term, in the long term, it leaves the issues unresolved. The people who have voted "against" still feel aggrieved, and the people who voted "for" may feel guilty about their "victory."

### Trap 5. Agreeing to disagree

This is a variant of Trap 4, and does not work for the same reason.

In general, take courage. Try the positive tactics in chapter four instead. They are far more likely to work.

# Creating common ground

A manager I know was giving a talk on how to understand financial data for non-financial specialists. The group seemed unusually attentive for such a dry subject. The reason was revealed later. They had opened a "book" with bets on how frequently he used two phrases: "The challenge before us is…" and "When I worked at…"

When talking to groups, you must not just mouth appropriate jargon, otherwise you will find yourself sounding like the "Random Mission Statement Generator" on the Internet, which produces meaningless phrases. Instead, you must learn to create common ground.

Effective influencers know how to persuade people through using the "pull" skill of creating common ground when you are talking to groups of people.

## Establishing your credibility

If you don't have credibility with your listeners, they will not pay attention to what you are saying. Many researchers have demonstrated this experimentally. In one experiment, an actor was hired to give a talk to groups. Some groups were told that he was a world-famous professor and an authority on the subject. Others

were told he was a student. Guess which groups found him more plausible? Where you have to persuade a group, it is vital to remind them of your credentials. In general, it is wise to tell the people you are addressing:

■  What you know of the subject
■  Why you are specially interested in it
■  What first-hand experience you have
■  What your general track record is

## Consulting

It is always useful to talk ahead of the meeting to key people who will be present. Ask them:

■  What they think of the subject under discussion
■  Why it matters to them
■  What advice they would give you about how to present the issue at the meeting
■  Whether there are any hidden traps to avoid

Use summarizing skills to check your understanding. Test your ideas tentatively, putting more emphasis on listening than on talking.

## Understanding the audience

Understanding your listeners is at the heart of successful persuading where groups are concerned, and it is one of the easiest aspects to overlook. It is easy to overlook because most of us get too wrapped up in our own concerns – nervousness, desire to get our message across, and so on. But it is essential to ask yourself the following critical questions:

- Who is going to be there?
- What do they already know?
- What do they need to know?
- What are their likely concerns?
- What's at stake here? How much does it matter to them what I say?
- What's the history here? Is there a history of poor relationships or sloppy service? If so, you will need to note it and perhaps even refer to it openly.

### Enthusiasm and passion

You must speak with enthusiasm, and it must be genuine. Successful influencers persuade by showing that they really care about the subject under debate. They are prepared to show real emotion and to say why the topic matters to them personally. For instance, a manager who was introducing his team to the unwelcome idea that they had to move offices told them in an atmosphere of initial hostility that turned to total, sympathetic attention, because he said:

- He really believed this was the best solution because all others had been explored and rejected.

- He really cared where the team was based and knew how much it mattered to everyone there.

- The new commute would be personally inconvenient for him, but he was prepared to do it because it was in the team's best interests.

- He was going to do everything in his power to ensure that the team had the equipment and furniture they needed.

- They would have an office-cooling party when they moved out and an office-warming party when they moved in.

- He was proud of the team and knew they would do everything they could to support him, just as he would do everything he could to support them.

## Creating common ground

In spite of this "difficult" message, he received a heartfelt ovation at the end of his announcement.

---

**TIPS FOR SHOWING YOUR ENTHUSIASM:**

- Smile; it infects your voice.
- Keep your head up.
- Look around the room, and engage everyone with eye contact.
- Practice using a strong voice. A weak and reedy voice will give the opposite effect than the one you want.

---

### Talk about the benefits

All sales people are taught this, but how often is it used effectively at work?

There is a big difference in persuasiveness between features and benefits. Features give the facts. Benefits show how I can profit from the feature.

Persuasive speaking and creating common ground means you know how to describe the benefits of whatever you are proposing. I once watched a manager making a case for setting up a single training department in an organization that had many rival departments, all competing with one another and duplicating their efforts. The manager concerned made the mistake of trying to support his case with features – research and data about how unsatisfactory the current situation was. He would have done far better to concentrate on the benefits to the organization of establishing one training unit: greater cost effectiveness, increased impact, greater attractiveness to high quality trainers; and so on.

### Telling stories

The most effective persuaders do not rely on facts, figures, and data. They tell stories and weave achievable dreams. The managing director of one well-known chain store has his own unique way of doing this. Perching informally on the edge of a table in the staff dining room, he asks groups of employees what are this week's messages from the customers. He listens carefully and then says, "Well, let me tell you about what I've seen at other stores in my travels. Yesterday, in Birmingham, a customer came up to me and said…"

He may then go on to draw an attractive verbal picture of how good the store could be potentially if the various ideas and proposals that were suggested to him were implemented.

**HINTS ON STORY TELLING AS A PERSUASIVE TECHNIQUE**

- Use "I." Quote what you have seen.
- Tell anecdotes from your personal experience.
- Describe what these anecdotes have meant for you.
- Even in the tiniest anecdote, have a beginning, middle, and an end. Use cliff-hangers if you can: leave the end of the story until the last part of your piece.

## Emphasize success

It's easy to criticize, and many managers are experts in the criticism game. We criticize because it often seems less dangerous to attack others first than to take our share of the blame or to describe what success would look like.

I worked on and off for a year as a consultant with a team whose shared feeling was that it preferred to work as separate individuals than as an interdependent group. It would have been easy for the manager concerned to lambaste the team; to tell its members how disappointed he was in them; and to imply that he, himself, was blameless. Instead, about half way through our work, he openly admitted that he had given mixed messages to the team and that there was a part of him, too, that liked to play solo.

Then, he did something no one who was there will ever forget. He showed a piece of an old documentary film. It was of a team of ace pilots who flew roped together. That, he said, was his image of how he wanted the team to be: a team of individual experts whose fates hung together with the highest possible degree of mutual trust.

As well as emphasizing success, remember the value of *celebrating* success. Look for opportunites to give parties to celebrate:
- The achievement of a target
- Anniversaries; for example, setting up the team
- The award of a contract
- An award for the team or a team member
- Getting through a difficult period at work.

## Creating common ground

### Hints on emphasizing success

- Describe how success would look, sound, and feel in an ideal but achievable future.
- Avoid blaming.
- Take your share of responsibility for what has gone wrong.
- Ask the group for help on achieving the ideal.

### Use simple language

Nothing cuts people off more quickly than using jargon and long words. Jargon is specialist language that alienates because it excludes. Long words detract from your message because they are more difficult to understand than short ones. Short ones are more vivid and, therefore, more memorable.

### Work on the basis of needs and concerns, not solutions.

Talking about your needs and those of others is always more compelling than trying to "sell" a prepackaged solution. For instance, if you are asking for support, a solution-based request would be:

**"I want you to agree to my proposal for creating a new system."**

A needs-based statement would be:
**"I need your support."**

Another solution-based example would be:
**"I want you to leave me alone; I'm feeling stressed out."**

A much more powerful needs-based thing to say would be:
**"I need autonomy and space."**

Similarly, always ask others what their needs and concerns are, rather than asking them what solution they propose. "What do you need from me?" is often a powerful and much-neglected question.

Remember to state your assumptions and to make your thinking as visible as possible to others. When you have something momentous to discuss with your boss or your team, don't expect them to fill in the gaps in your sentences.

**ALWAYS EXPLAIN:**

■ What your basic assumptions are

■ What led up to them – how you formed them

■ What evidence you have to support them

And then invite others to question your assumptions by asking questions such as:

■ This is what I think, but how does it strike you?

■ What flaws can you see in this?

■ Where do you think the weak points are?

Like much of the best strategy on influencing, it may seem as if you are exposing a weakness; but actually you are operating from a position of strength. Having the confidence to invite others to test your conclusions is one of the best ways to ensure that you create common ground. It gets objections out into the open and allows you to help others make their thinking visible to you.

# The wider scene

### Networking, influencing upward, values

A few years ago, I worked with a senior manager who felt that her career had come to a frustrating halt. She wanted to get to the next tier in her organization because she felt she had a lot to offer. This was a large, global company, so the next tier meant a very senior job, indeed. What was holding her back?

Everyone agreed that she was a spendid manager. Her staff admired her. She had done excellent work in all of her international assignments. It did not take a lot of investigation to establish that the problem was networking. Inside her department she was known and influential. Outside of it she was hardly known at all. In terms of influencing, she needed to develop and learn the key skill of networking.

Skillful networking is an essential part of skillful influencing. As you climb the corporate ladder, far more of your work will have to do with working upwards and outwards.

For instance, Ben is a computer specialist. He works for a young company and was hired for his software expertise. Three years ago he was in his first managerial role and was responsible for a small team of six people. He still did a little operational work himself. Apart from his boss, his main daily contact was with his team. He rarely needed to get involved with the wider scene in his organization.

Today, Ben is running a 12-person team. He has no time now for hands-on software development because a great deal of his time is spent in meetings. Increasingly, he is responsible for developing some aspects of company strategy in his division. He is expected to meet important clients, go to conferences, present occasional papers at the senior team meeting, and so on.

If Ben's career continues as expected, his next job will involve even more of his time being spent on networking outside the company.

### Working outside the organization

At the most senior level, the Chief Executive Officer of an organization may spend the majority of his or her time working outside the organization itself, influencing politicians, suppliers, and keeping accounts.

This is just the reality of life in organizations today. You cannot be self-sufficient. You need the active co-operation and support of people in other parts of the organization. The formal diagram of the organization chart never actually represents the way power and influence work in organizations. The informal networks are just as powerful, and these don't recognize any boundaries. The most influential managers in organizations know how to use both the formal and the informal channels of information and influence.

Here's a checklist to help you evaluate your current networking skill:

| DO YOU NETWORK? | Never | Sometimes | Often |
|---|---|---|---|
| I have lunch with people from other departments. | | | |
| I go to conferences. | | | |
| I am in contact with people in my field from other organizations. | | | |
| People in other departments contact me for advice and information. | | | |
| I am asked to join task forces or project teams outside my immediate area of expertise. | | | |
| I go to social events in the organization outside those of my immediate team. | | | |
| My boss's colleagues know me well and chat to me when they see me. | | | |
| I use the Internet to make contacts in my field. | | | |
| I hear reliable information about new developments in my organization before most other people do. | | | |

## Where did you put most of your checks?

**Never:** It's your choice. If you want to remain a specialist, then fine. If you want to broaden your range of influence, then read this section carefully.

**Sometimes:** You will already be doing a lot of the right things. Use this section to consider some new ideas.

**Often:** You are already networking well. Use this section as a reminder of how useful it is.

## The wider scene

### The favor bank

Networking works on the banking principle, where the currency is favors. The favor can be information, a task, advice, or a recommendation. You do a favor for someone else, and you have credit in their account. They do a favor for you, and they have credit in yours. Each side may make withdrawals over a period of time. As long as there is a rough balance in the account, it works well for both sides.

The favor bank is at its most useful when it operates outside your immediate professional environment; because this is where you will hear of people, information, and ideas beyond the daily exchange of information in your team. If you do not have a favor bank, is it likely that you are networking effectively?

### Creating a network

#### 1. Map your network

First, draw your exisiting network as a spider diagram. What gaps does this reveal? What's the balance between contacts inside your team, outside it, and outside your organization? Where are the strengths?

#### 2. Joining a task force

Make it clear to your boss and other senior managers that you are open to joining a task force or project team that has a remit beyond that of your current responsibilities. Joining a task force is a good idea because:

- People who join task forces show their willingness to think beyond immediate self-interest. They have shown that they are ready to sacrifice time and energy for the sake of the wider good.
- You are exposed to ideas from beyond your immediate team as well as ideas from leading-edge thinkers in your field.
- It brings you to the attention of more senior people.

### 3. Socialize

World-weary cynicism is often fashionable in organizations. Try to resist it. If your organization runs cross-functional workshops to update you on what is going on, attend them. If there are Christmas parties and summer picnics, go. Social encounters are golden opportunities to extend your range of acquaintances and build your network.

### 4. Find a mentor

A mentor is an older, wiser person in the organization who is not your line manager and is probably in a different department. The idea is that the mentor is not in competition with you and has reached the stage in his or her career where they are willing to pass on ideas and help. You and the mentor meet regularly for two hours or so at a time and discuss issues that are bothering you. Confidentiality is guaranteed; mentors don't gossip.

## 5. Get on training courses

Training courses are an excellent way to meet people beyond your usual network. Try to mix internal with external courses. If all you ever go on are your organization's own courses, you will find that you share the same enthusiasms but also the same blind spots as others. Spending a long time in one organization is a sure route to forgetting how weird its funny little ways seemed to you when you first joined. Meeting people from other organizations is a way of immunizing yourself against blind spots becoming a permanent handicap.

## 6. Trade journals and conferences

Similarly, make sure you read the trade journals and go regularly to conferences in your field. The trade journals will always contain announcements about the important conferences.

## 7. Join a learning team

A learning team is a group of up to eight people, usually from a range of organizations (though they can be from different parts of one large organization) often with a professional facilitator. There is no formal agenda. Each person has an agreed amount of time to explore any issue of concern to him or her. The set usually meets for a day at a time. The idea is that, by learning to listen and question carefully, every participant learns a great deal not only about the issues but also about himself. Relationships quickly become close. Such teams are also powerfully useful networks. Long after the six or eight meetings that most teams have, the members are in touch and know that they can call on one another for help.

## Influencing upward

Many relatively new managers do not appreciate that one of their prime tasks is to manage their manager. Mostly, this is because they think of management as being about managing downward. In fact, it is just as important to manage upward. If you neglect this, you will be neglecting one of the prime ways you can be influential in the organization and cutting yourself off from one of your main sources of help and advice. This may seem like odd advice if you:

- Are in awe of your boss
- Are afraid of him or her
- Don't respect him or her.

## The wider scene

No matter how you feel about your boss, it is still part of your job to manage him or her effectively. If you are not doing this now, here are some ideas:

- Talk to your boss about his or her aspirations for the department.
- Ask how you can help achieve them.
- Find out, within the limits of courtesy, what your boss's personal situation is – married, single, with or without children and other commitments?
- Find out what his or her leisure interests are and share some of your own interests.
- How does your boss like to be influenced? If you don't know, ask.
- Ask for feedback on your style, strengths, and weaknesses as you boss sees them.
- If appropriate, offer your boss feedback on how he or she strikes you.
- Offer your support and loyalty.

### Be a problem solver

In general, the way to manage upward is to position yourself as a problem solver, not a problem creator. Some ideas for influencing upward more efffectively might include:

- Never make a criticism or raise a problem without offering a solution, especially one that does not involve spending a lot more money or hiring extra people. For instance, you might say, "*Our phone lines are constantly busy, and I've had feedback from customers that they can't get through. What I suggest is that we add another two lines. I've looked at the cost, and it would be small. What do you think?*"
- Make sure your suggestions and ideas are linked to benefits for the organization, and point these out.
- Keep yourself well informed about the more strategic issues that will be disturbing more senior managers. Refer to these in conversations with your boss.
- Never, ever refer to more senior managers as "The Management," as in, "*The Management won't let us do x or y.*" They find this discourteous, and it lumps all bosses together – something bosses hate. It also suggests that the speaker sees bosses as a different breed from everyone else.

### Small talk

Networking can be a nightmare for people who are shy or who hate the apparent triviality of small talk. Fortunately, there is a simple solution. It is well described by Dale Carnegie in his book *How to Win Friends and Influence People*. He describes sitting next to a distinguished botanist at a dinner party. He had never met the man before. At the end of the evening, the botanist thanked Carnegie and praised him as a stimulating conversationalist, despite the fact that he had hardly said a word all evening, as he knew nothing about botany. In reality, Carnegie had been a good listener and had encouraged the botanist to talk.

Listening carefully and with rapport, asking the occasional question, and summarizing (see pages 38 – 50) is the answer to the shy person's fear of small talk. Most of us love talking about our interests and are only too delighted to talk away to someone who will listen.

### Walking the talk

A client was describing a recent dilemma. He runs a small company and had discovered that the company had underpaid its sales tax. Because of some quirk in the way this had come about, there was no way that this underpayment could have been discovered. He and his colleagues had spent part of their team meeting discussing it. They had no real difficulty in deciding what to do. Why? Because, as a group, they had spent some time agreeing on their core values as a company. This included a commitment to abiding by the law.

As my client said, *"There's no point in having a list of values if they remain a list. You've got to walk the talk."* The company

contacted the Collector of Revenue and paid their sales tax. If they had not done so, what would the consequences have been? Clearly, none, legally. But morally there would have been many. The message would have been that it was OK to cheat. The OK-to-cheat message could soon have been passed on to dealings with clients, suppliers, and employees.

### Establishing ground rules

Influential people in organizations are clear about their own values and beliefs and talk about them openly and passionately. They establish ground rules that relate to ideal and better ways of behaving, rather than to bureaucratic rules and regulations. They reward people whom they see behaving in these ways and are consistent themselves about trying to practice what they preach. A manager or leader who is perceived to lack integrity may have vision and courage; but, without integrity, he or she is lost.

## The wider scene

### Your own core values

What would you consider to be your own personal core values? What would cause you to resign? If you don't know, think about and write down some answers to these questions:

**What is important to you about what you do professionally?**


**What would you rather be doing if you were not doing what you currently do professionally?**


**What is it about what you would rather be doing that is important to you?**


**Who are your heroes or heroines? Who do you admire – living, dead, or fictional?**


**What is it about this person/these people that you admire?**


**Looking back at your answers, what values does this exercise indicate you have?**

The question now is, how do you allow your core values to show through what you do? This question is closely linked to another important question: How do you create trust? Others people's trust is easily destroyed but not so easily acquired. It is one of the most fragile and one of the most important qualities you can have if you are to influence others.

## Here are some suggestions:

■ Tell people what your values are. Having told them, model those values in what you do; walk the talk. For instance, if you say that one of your values is equal opportunities, then ensure that when you promote people it is on the basis of mind, not prejudice or favoritism.

■ Share all the information you have. Many organizations mistakenly believe their staff cannot handle sensitive information and so restrict its availability. In fact, if you do not share information, the grapevine will fill in the gaps with rumor. Tell people what you know, even when there is nothing to report. For example, say, "There are no new developments, but I'll tell you the moment I hear anything."

■ Under-promise and over-perform rather than over-promise and under-perform. If you say you'll do something, deliver on the promise.

■ Own up to mistakes. Many organizations, with their culture of blame, discourage people from acknowledging their errors; but it is vital for trust. If you admit it when you have done something wrong, you will encourage your team to do the same. Innovation comes from risk, and risk involves making occasional mistakes.

■ Adhere to the values and ethics of your profession, organization, or team. If your team does not have its own list of values, spend some time working on one at an off-site or extended team meeting. Don't just leave it at the list. Ask the team to identify what you'd all be doing if you were behaving in a way that reflects you and then regularly monitor how you are all performing against that list of values and behavior.

■ If you feel you face an ethical dilemma, use team meetings to discuss it openly. Encourage the team to do the same and consult more senior managers if necessary.

**Take some time out with your team to establish your team values. Do not deal with this issue at a standard meeting. Ask your team these questions:**
■ **What do we want our customers, bosses, the rest of our staff, and the media to say about us?**
■ **What behavior do we need to ensure that they say these things?**
■ **What values does this suggest we must have?**
■ **How will we make sure we stick to these values in our everyday work?**

# Action planning

Reading this book may have stimulated your ideas on how you could become more effective at influencing. Writing down some actual goals for translating ideas into action can increase the chances that you will act, rather than just have good intentions.

Use these pages to jot down what you plan to do.

**1.** What feedback have you already had about your influencing style? What are the main points people have made to you?

| Boss | Team/clients | Friends and family |
| --- | --- | --- |
| | | |
| | | |
| | | |

**2.** Getting feedback from others about how they see you is one of the most useful ways to improve.
Remember the wise words of the Scottish poet Robert Burns,

*"Would that God the gift would gie us/To see oursels as others see us."*
Take some time to think about how you can increase the amount of feedback you currently receive.

| SOME IDEAS | YOUR NOTES |
| --- | --- |
| 1. Ask five or six people who know you well, the following questions: In what ways am I already effective at influencing? How could I be more effective? | |
| 2. Go to a course where you get feedback from fellow participants and instructors. | |
| 3. Distribute a questionnaire that gives you anonymous "360 degree feedback" from a range of colleagues, always with a facilitator or coach to discuss and interpret the results. | |

**3.** Give feedback to yourself. In reading through this book, where do you feel your strengths are, and where are the areas for development?

| "PULL" LEVERS | Strengths | Development areas |
|---|---|---|
| Creating rapport | | |
| Listening | | |
| Questioning | | |
| "PUSH" LEVERS | | |
| Asking for what you want | | |
| Saying "no" | | |
| Giving feedback | | |
| "PUSH AND PULL" SKILLS | | |
| Creating common ground | | |
| The wider scene: networking, influencing upward, values | | |

**4.** Overall, what action should you take to effectively build on the strengths and diminish the weaknesses?

Who else needs to be involved? Think carefully about what actual outcomes you want and how you would know if you had achieved that outcome. For instance, going to a seminar is not an outcome, because you can take a course and still not have improved your skills in a practical way, though you increase the chances of improvement. Taking a course is only a means to improving skills; it is not an end in itself.

| Goal | How you plan to achieve it | Who else needs to be involved | Target date for completion |
|---|---|---|---|
| | | | |
| | | | |
| | | | |
| | | | |
| | | | |
| | | | |

# Index

**If you liked Influencing People by Jenny Rogers check out these other great career-building books from AMACOM.**

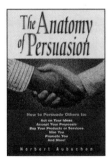

### Anatomy of Persuasion
**How to Persuade Others to Act on Your Ideas, Accept Your Proposals, Buy Your Products or Services, Hire You, Promote You, and More**

*Norbert Aubuchon*

Some people seem able to talk anybody into anything. This book provides you with a unique and proven analytical thinking process that you can use to analyze, organize, and present information in a persuasive way -- and get what you want!

$17.95   Order #7952-XBKM   ISBN: 0-8144-7952-9

### Say What Your Mean, Get What Your Want
**A Businessperson's Guide to Direct Communication**

*Judith C. Tingley, PhD.*

If you want people to pay attention when you speak, then assertive communication should be your goal. This book explores a variety of business situations, including: giving and getting feedback; expressing opinions; asking for what you want; dealing with rejection; delegation; and expecting accountability.

$15.95   Order #7904-XBKM   ISBN: 0-8144-7904-9

### How to Negotiate Anything with Anyone, Anywhere Around the World, new expanded edition.
*Frank L. Acuff*

"With comprehensive background material on the histories, customs, and economies of numerous countries, this primer is a must for the business traveler." -- Entepreneur

$21.95   Order #7950-XBKM   ISBN: 0-8144-7950-2

### The Negotiation Tool Kit
**How to Get Exactly What You Want in Any Business or Personal Situation**

*Roger J. Volkema*

A fresh new approach to mastering negotiation skills, this book is a hands-on workbook that integrates questions and answers, self-assessments, mini-surveys, feedback measures, and action challenges to help you build personal confidence and negotiation prowess. You will learn the "golden rule" of negotiation, three fundamental questions of negotiation, when not to negotiate, eight behaviors of star negotiators, and more.

$17.95   Order #8008-XBKM   ISBN: 0-8144-8008-x

## Call 1-800-262-9699 or order in your local bookstore.